Coding

for
dummies®

W9-AFT-494

Coding

for
dummies®
A Wiley Brand

by Nikhil Abraham

for
dummies®
A Wiley Brand

Coding For Dummies®

Published by: **John Wiley & Sons, Inc.**, 111 River Street, Hoboken, NJ 07030-5774, www.wiley.com

For general information on our other products and services, please contact our Customer Care Department within the U.S. at 877-762-2974, outside the U.S. at 317-572-3993, or fax 317-572-4002. For technical support, please visit www.wiley.com/techsupport.

Wiley publishes in a variety of print and electronic formats and by print-on-demand. Some material included with standard print versions of this book may not be included in e-books or in print-on-demand. If this book refers to media such as a CD or DVD that is not included in the version you purchased, you may download this material at http://booksupport.wiley.com. For more information about Wiley products, visit www.wiley.com.

Library of Congress Control Number: 2014954659

ISBN 978-1-119-29332-3 (pbk); ISBN 978-1-119-29610-2 (ebk); ISBN 978-1-119-29607-2 (ebk)

Coding For Dummies (9781119293323) was previously published as Coding For Dummies (9781118951309). While this version features a new Dummies cover and design, the content is the same as the prior release and should not be considered a new or updated product.

Manufactured in the United States of America

10 9 8 7 6 5 4 3 2

Contents at a Glance

Table of Contents

Introduction

The ability to read, write, and understand code has never been more important, useful, or lucrative as it is today. Computer code has forever changed our lives. Some people can't even make it through the day without interacting with something built with code. Even so, for many people, the world of coding seems complex and inaccessible. Maybe you participated in a tech-related business meeting and did not fully understand the conversation. Perhaps you tried to build a web page for your family and friends, but ran into problems displaying pictures or aligning text. Maybe you're even intimidated by the unrecognizable words on the covers of books about coding: words such as HTML, CSS, JavaScript, Python, or Ruby.

If you've previously been in these situations, then *Coding For Dummies* is for you. This book explains basic concepts so you can participate in technical conversations, and ask the right questions. Don't worry — in this book I've assumed you are starting with little to no previous coding knowledge, and I haven't tried to cram every possible coding concept into these pages. Additionally, I encourage you here to learn by doing, and by actually creating your own programs. Instead of a website, imagine that you wanted to build a house. You could spend eight years studying to be an architect, or you could start today by learning a little bit about foundations and framing. This book kickstarts your coding journey today.

The importance of coding is ever increasing. As author and technologist Douglas Rushkoff famously said, "program or be programmed." When humans invented languages and then the alphabet, people learned to listen and speak, and then read and write. In our increasingly digital world, it is important to learn not just how to use programs, but how to make them as well. For example, observe this transition in music. For over a century, music labels decided what songs the public could listen to and purchase. In 2005, three coders created YouTube, which allowed anyone to release songs. Today more songs have been uploaded to YouTube than have been released by all the record labels in the last century combined.

Accompanying this book are examples at www.codecademy.com, whose exercises are one of the easiest ways to learn how to code without installing or downloading anything. The Codecademy companion site includes examples and exercises from this book, along with projects and examples for additional practice.

About This Book

This book is designed for readers with little to no coding experience, and gives an overview of programming to non-programmers. In plain English, you learn how code is used to create web programs, who makes those programs, and the processes they use. The topics covered include:

>> Explaining what coding is and answering the common questions related to code.

>> Building basic websites using the three most common languages: HTML, CSS, and JavaScript.

>> Surveying other programming languages such as Ruby and Python.

>> Building an application using everything you learn in the book.

As you read this book, keep the following in mind:

>> The book can be read from beginning to end, but feel free to skip around if you like. If any topic interests you, start there. You can always return to the previous chapter, if necessary.

>> At some point you will get stuck, and code you write will not work as intended. Do not fear! There are many resources to help you including support forums, others on the Internet, and me! Using Twitter, you can send me a public message at @nikhilgabraham with the hashtag #codingFD.

>> Code in the book will appear in a monospaced font like this: `<h1>Hi there! </h1>`.

Foolish Assumptions

I do not make many assumptions about you, the reader, but I do make a few:

I assume you don't have previous programming experience. To follow along, then, you only need to be able to read, type, and follow directions. I try to explain as many concepts as possible using examples and analogies you already know.

I assume you have a computer running the latest version of Google Chrome. The examples in the book have been tested and optimized for the Chrome browser, which is available for free from Google. Even so, the examples may also work in the latest version of Firefox. Using Internet Explorer for the examples in this book, however, is discouraged.

I assume you have access to an Internet connection. Some of the examples in the book can be done without an Internet connection, but most require one so you can access and complete the exercises on www.codecademy.com.

Icons Used in This Book

Here are the icons used in the book to flag text that should be given extra attention or can be skipped.

TIP

This icon flags useful information or explains a shortcut to help you understand a concept.

TECHNICAL STUFF

This icon explains technical details about the concept being explained. The details might be informative or interesting, but are not essential to your understanding of the concept at this stage.

REMEMBER

Try not to forget the material marked with this icon. It signals an important concept or process that you should keep in mind.

WARNING

Watch out! This icon flags common mistakes and problems that can be avoided if you heed the warning.

Beyond the Book

A lot of extra content that you won't find in this book is available at www.dummies.com. Go online to find the following:

>> **The source code for the examples in this book and a link to the Codecademy exercises:** You can find these at

    www.dummies.com/go/codingfd

The source code is organized by chapter. The best way to work with a chapter is to download all the source code for it at one time.

>> **Cheat Sheet:** You can find a list of common HTML, CSS, and JavaScript commands, among other useful information, at

To view this book's Cheat Sheet, simply go to www.dummies.com and search for "Coding For Dummies Cheat Sheet" in the Search box.

>> **Extras:** Additional articles with extra content are posted for roughly each section of the book. You can access these additional materials at

```
www.dummies.com/extras/coding
```

>> **Updates:** Code and specifications are constantly changing, so the commands and syntax that work today may not work tomorrow. You can find any updates or corrections by visiting

```
www.dummies.com/extras/coding
```

Where to Go from Here

All right, now that all of the administrative stuff is out of the way, it's time to get started. You can totally do this. Congratulations on taking your first step into the world of coding!

1
Getting Started with Coding

Chapter 1

What Is Coding?

"A million dollars isn't cool, you know what's cool? A billion dollars."
— SEAN PARKER, THE SOCIAL NETWORK

Every week the newspapers report on another technology company that has raised capital or sold for millions of dollars. Sometimes, in the case of companies like Instagram, WhatsApp, and Uber, the amount in the headline is for billions of dollars. These articles may pique your curiosity, and you may want to see how code is used to build the applications that experience these financial outcomes. Alternatively, your interests may lie closer to work. Perhaps you work in an industry in decline, like print media, or in a function that technology is rapidly changing, like marketing. Whether you are thinking about switching to a new career or improving your current career, understanding computer programming or "coding" can help with your professional development. Finally, your interest may be more personal — perhaps you have an idea, a burning desire to create something, a website or an app, to solve a problem you have experienced, and you know reading and writing code is the first step to building your solution. Whatever your motivation, this book will shed light on coding and programmers, and help you think of both not as mysterious and complex but approachable and something you can do yourself.

In this chapter, you will understand what code is, what industries are affected by computer software, the different types of programming languages used to write code, and take a tour of a web app built with code.

Defining What Code Is

Computer code is not a cryptic activity reserved for geniuses and oracles. In fact, in a few minutes you will be writing some computer code yourself! Most computer code performs a range of tasks in our lives from the mundane to the extraordinary. Code runs our traffic lights and pedestrian signals, the elevators in our buildings, the cell phone towers that transmit our phone signals, and the space ships headed for outer space. We also interact with code on a more personal level, on our phones and computers, and usually to check email or the weather.

Following instructions

Computer code is a set of statements, like sentences in English, and each statement directs the computer to perform a single step or instruction. Each of these steps is very precise, and followed to the letter. For example, if you are in a restaurant and ask a waiter to direct you to the restroom, he might say, "head to the back, and try the middle door." To a computer, these directions are so vague as to be unusable. Instead, if the waiter gave instructions to you as if you were a computer program he might say, "From this table, walk northeast for 40 paces. Then turn right 90 degrees, walk 5 paces, turn left 90 degrees, and walk 5 paces. Open the door directly in front of you, and enter the restroom." Figure 1-1 shows lines of code from the popular game, Pong. Do not worry about trying to understand what every single line does, or feel intimated. You will soon be reading and writing your own code.

```
1  launchPong(function () {
2      function colour_random() {
3          var num = Math.floor(Math.random() * Math.pow(2, 24));
4          return '#' + ('00000' + num.toString(16)).substr(-6);
5      }
6
7
8      pongSettings.ball.size = 15;
9      pongSettings.ball.color = colour_random();
10     pongSettings.ball.velocity[0] = 15;
11     pongSettings.ball.velocity[1] = 15;
12
13  });
14
15
```

FIGURE 1-1:
Computer code from the game Pong.

One rough way to measure a program's complexity is to count its statements or lines of code. Basic applications like the Pong game have 5,000 lines of code, while more complex applications like Facebook currently have over 10 million lines of code. Whether few or many lines of code, the computer follows each instruction exactly and effortlessly, never tiring like the waiter might when asked for the 100th time for the location of the restroom.

Be careful of only using lines of code as a measure for a program's complexity. Just like when writing in English, 100 well written lines of code can perform the same functionality as 1,000 poorly written lines of code.

Writing code with some Angry Birds

If you have never written code before, now is your chance to try! Go to `http://csedweek.org/learn` and under the heading "Tutorials for Beginners" click the "Write Your First Computer Program" link with the Angry Birds icon, as shown in Figure 1-2. This tutorial is meant for those with no previous computer programming experience, and introduces the basic building blocks used by all computer programs. The most important take-away from the tutorial is to understand that computer programs use code to literally and exactly tell the computer to execute a set of instructions.

FIGURE 1-2:
Write your first computer program with a game-like tutorial using Angry Birds.

Computer Science Education Week is an annual program dedicated to elevating the profile of computer science during one week in December. In the past, President Obama, Bill Gates, basketball player Chris Bosh, and singer Shakira, among others, have supported and encouraged people from the US and around the world to participate.

Understanding What Coding Can Do for You

Coding can be used to perform tasks and solve problems that you experience every day. The "everyday" situations in which programs or apps can provide assistance continues to grow at an exponential pace, but this was not always the case. The rise of web applications, internet connectivity, and mobile phones have inserted software programs into daily life, and lowered the barrier for you to become a creator, solving personal and professional problems with code.

Eating the world with software

In 2011, Marc Andreessen, creator of Netscape Navigator and now venture capitalist, noted that "software is eating the world." He predicted that software companies would disrupt existing companies at a rapid pace. Traditionally, code powered software used on desktops and laptops. The software had to first be installed, and then you had to supply data to the program. Three trends have dramatically increased the use of code in everyday life:

>> **Web-based software:** This software operates in the browser without requiring installation. For example, if you wanted to check your email, you previously had to install an email client either by downloading the software or from a CD-ROM. Sometimes, issues arose when the software was not available for your operating system, or conflicted with your operating system version. Hotmail, a web-based email client, rose to popularity, in part, because it allowed users visiting www.hotmail.com to instantly check their email without worrying about installation or software compatibility. Web applications increased consumer appetite to try more applications, and developers in turn were incentivized to write more applications.

>> **Internet broadband connectivity:** Broadband connectivity has increased, providing a fast Internet connection to more people in the last few years than in the previous decade. Today, more than two billion people can access web-based software, up from approximately 50 million only a decade ago.

>> **Mobile phones:** Today's smartphones bring programs with you wherever you go, and help supply data to programs. Many software programs became more useful when accessed on-the-go than when limited to a desktop computer. For instance, use of maps applications greatly increased thanks to mobile phones because users need directions the most when lost, not just when planning a trip at home on the computer. In addition, mobile phones are equipped with sensors that measure and supply data to programs like orientation, acceleration, and current location through GPS. Now instead of having to input all the data to programs yourself, mobile devices can help. For instance, a fitness application like RunKeeper does not require you to input start and end times to keep track of your runs. You can press start at the beginning of your run, and the phone will automatically track your distance, speed, and time.

The combination of these trends have created software companies that have upended incumbents in almost every industry, especially ones typically immune to technology. Some notable examples include:

>> **Airbnb:** Airbnb is a peer-to-peer lodging company that owns no rooms, yet books more nights than the Hilton and Intercontinental, the largest hotel chains in the world. (See Figure 1-3.)

>> **Uber:** Uber is a car transportation company that owns no vehicles, books more trips, and has more drivers in the largest 200 cities than any other car or taxi service.

>> **Groupon:** Groupon, the daily deals company, generated almost $1 billion after just two years in business, growing faster than any other company in history, let alone any other traditional direct marketing company.

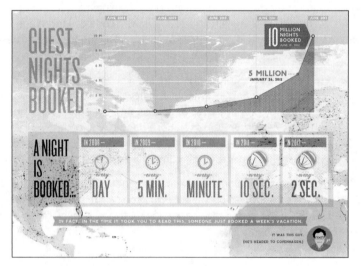

FIGURE 1-3
Airbnb booked 5 million nights after 3.5 years, and its next 5 million nights 6 months later.

Coding on the job

Coding can be useful in the workplace as well. Outside the technology sector, coding in the workplace is common for some professions like financial traders, economists, and scientists. However, for most professionals outside the technology sector, coding is just beginning to penetrate the workplace, and gradually starting to increase in relevance. Here are areas where coding is playing a larger role on the job:

>> **Advertising:** Spend is shifting from print and TV to digital campaigns, and search engine advertising and optimization relies on keywords to bring visitors to websites. Advertisers who understand code see successful keywords used by competitors, and use that data to create more effective campaigns.

>> **Marketing:** When promoting products, personalizing communication is one strategy that often increases results. Marketers who code can query customer databases and create personalized communications that include customer names and products tailored to specific interests.

>> **Sales:** The sales process always starts with leads. Salespeople who code retrieve their own leads from web pages and directories, and then sort and quality those leads.

TIP

Retrieving information by copying text on web pages and in directories is referred to as *scraping*.

>> **Design:** After creating a web page or a digital design, designers must persuade other designers and eventually developers to actually program their drawings into the product. Designers who code can more easily bring their designs to life, and can more effectively advocate for specific designs by creating working prototypes that others can interact with.

>> **Public relations:** Companies constantly measure how customers and the public react to announcements and news. For instance, if a celebrity spokesperson for a company does or says something offensive, should the company dump the celebrity? Public relations people who code query social media networks like Twitter or Facebook, and analyze hundreds of thousands of individual messages to understand market sentiment.

>> **Operations:** Additional profit can be generated, in part, by analyzing a company's costs. Operations people who code write programs to try millions of combinations to optimize packaging methods, loading routines, and delivery routes.

Scratching your own itch (and becoming rich and famous)

Using code built by others and coding in the workplace may cause you to think of problems you personally face that you could solve with code of your own. You may have an idea for a social network website, a better fitness app, or something new altogether. The path from idea to functioning prototype used by others involves a good amount of time and work, but might be more achievable than you think. For example, take Coffitivity, a productivity website that streams ambient coffee shop sounds to create white noise. The website was created by two people who had just learned how to program a few months prior. Shortly after Coffitivity launched, Time Magazine named the website one of 50 Best Websites of 2013, and the Wall

Street Journal also reviewed the website. While not every startup or app will initially receive this much media coverage, it can be helpful to know what is possible when a solution really solves a problem.

Having a goal, like a website or app you want to build, is one of the best ways to learn how to code. When facing a difficult bug or a hard concept, the idea of bringing your website to life will provide the motivation you need to keep going. Just as important, do not learn how to code to become rich and famous, as the probability of your website or app becoming successful is largely due to factors out of your control.

TIP

The characteristics that make a website or app addictive are described using the Hook Model here http://techcrunch.com/2012/03/04/how-to-manufacture-desire. Products are usually made by companies, and the characteristics of an enduring company are described here http://www.sequoiacap.com/grove/posts/yal6/elements-of-enduring-companies, based on a review of companies funded by Sequoia, one of the most successful venture capital firms in the world and early investors in Apple, Google, and PayPal.

Surveying the Types of Programming Languages

Code comes in different flavors called *programming languages.* Some popular programing languages are shown in Figure 1-4.

FIGURE 1-4: Some popular programming languages.

You can think of programming languages just like spoken languages, as they both share many of the same characteristics, such as:

>> **Functionality across languages:** Programming languages can all create the same functionality similar to how spoken languages can all express the same objects, phrases, and emotions.

>> **Syntax and structure:** Commands in programming languages can overlap just like words in spoken languages overlap. To output text to screen in Python or Ruby you use the `print` command, just like imprimer and imprimir are the verbs for "print" in French and Spanish.

>> **Natural lifespan:** Programming languages are born when a programmer thinks of a new or easier way to express a computational concept. If other programmers agree, they adopt the language for their own programs and the programming language spreads. However, just like Latin or Aramaic, if the programming language is not adopted by other programmers or a better language comes along, then the programming language slowly dies from lack of use.

Despite these similarities, programming languages also differ from spoken languages in a few key ways:

>> **One creator:** Unlike spoken languages, programming languages can be created by one person in a short period of time, sometimes in just a few days. Popular languages with a single creator include JavaScript (Brendan Eich), Python (Guido van Rossum), and Ruby (Yukihiro Matsumoto).

>> **Written in English:** Unlike spoken languages (except, of course, English), almost all programming languages are written in English. Whether they're programming in HTML, JavaScript, Python, or Ruby, Brazilian, French, or Chinese programmers all use the same English keywords and syntax in their code. Some non-English programming languages exist, such as languages in Hindi or Arabic, but none of these languages are widespread or mainstream.

Comparing low-level and high-level programming languages

One way to classify programming languages is either as low-level languages or high-level languages. Low-level languages interact directly with the computer processor or CPU, are capable of performing very basic commands, and are generally hard to read. Machine code, one example of a low-level language, uses code that consists of just two numbers — 0 and 1. Figure 1-5 shows an example of machine code. Assembly language, another low-level language, uses keywords to perform basic commands like read data, move data, and store data.

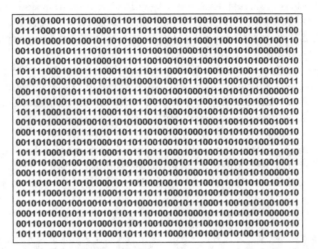

FIGURE 1-5: Machine code consists of 0s and 1s.

By contrast, high-level languages use natural language so it is easier for people to read and write. Once code is written in a high-level language, like C++, Python, or Ruby, an interpreter or compiler translates this high-level language into low-level code a computer can understand.

Contrasting compiled code and interpreted code

High-level programming languages must be converted to low-level programming languages using an interpreter or compiler, depending on the language. Interpreted languages are considered more portable than compiled languages, while compiled languages execute faster than interpreted languages. However, the speed advantage compiled languages have is starting to fade in importance as improving processor speeds make performance differences between interpreted and compiled languages negligible.

High-level programming languages like JavaScript, Python, and Ruby are interpreted. For these languages the interpreter executes the program directly, translating each statement *one line at a time* into machine code. High-level programming languages like C++, COBOL, and Visual Basic are compiled. For these languages, after the code is written a compiler translates *all* the code into machine code, and an executable file is created. This executable file is then distributed via the internet, CD-ROMs, or other media and run. Software you install on your computer, like Microsoft Windows or Mac OS X, are coded using compiled languages, usually C or C++.

Programming for the web

Software accessible on websites is gradually starting to take over installed software. Think of the last time you downloaded and installed software for your computer — you may not even remember! Installed software like Windows Media Player and Winamp that play music and movies have been replaced with websites like YouTube and Netflix. Traditional installed word processor and spreadsheet software like Microsoft Word and Excel are starting to see competition from web software like Google Docs and Sheets. Google is even selling laptops called Chromebooks that contain no installed software, and instead rely exclusively on web software to provide functionality.

The remainder of this book will focus on developing and creating web software, not just because web software is growing rapidly, but also because programs for the web are easier to learn and launch than traditional installed software.

Taking a Tour of a Web App Built with Code

With all this talk of programming, let us actually take a look at a web application built with code. Yelp.com is a website that allows you to search and find crowd-sourced reviews for local businesses like restaurants, nightlife, and shopping. As shown in Figure 1-6, Yelp did not always look as polished as it does today, but its purpose has stayed relatively constant over the years.

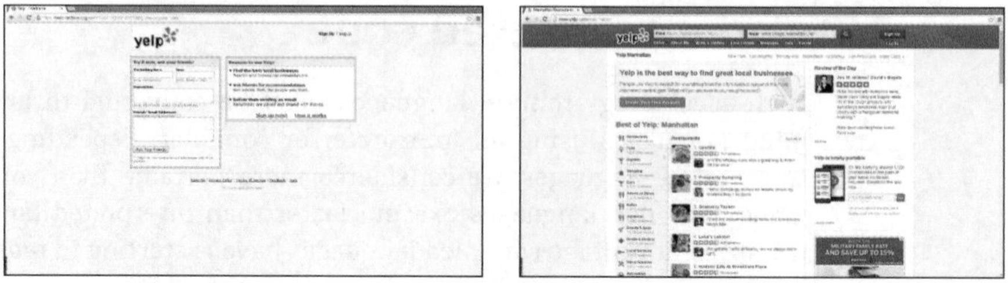

FIGURE 1-6:
Yelp's website in 2004 and in 2014.

Defining the app's purpose and scope

Once you understand an app's purpose, you can identify a few actionable tasks a user should be able to perform to achieve that purpose. Regardless of design, the Yelp's website has always allowed users to

>> Search local listings based on venue type and location.

>> Browse listing results for address, hours, reviews, photos, and location on a map.

Successful web applications generally allow for completing only a few key tasks when using the app. Adding too many features to an app is called scope creep, dilutes the strength of the existing features, and so is avoided by most developers. For example, it took Yelp, which has 30,000 restaurant reviews, exactly one decade after its founding to allow users to make reservations at those restaurants directly on its website. Whether you are using or building an app, have a clear sense of the app's purpose.

Standing on the shoulders of giants

Developers make strategic choices and decide which parts of the app to code themselves, and which parts of the app to use code built by others. Developers often turn to 3rd party providers for functionality that is either not core to the business or not an area of strength. In this way, apps stand on the shoulders of others, and benefit from others who have come before and solved challenging problems.

Yelp, for instance, displays local listing reviews and places every listing on a map. While Yelp solicits the reviews, and writes the code to display basic listing data, it is Google, as shown in Figure 1-7, which develops the maps used on Yelp's website. By using Google's map application instead of building its own, Yelp created the first version of the app with fewer engineers than otherwise would have been required.

FIGURE 1-7: Google maps used for the Yelp web application.

IN THIS CHAPTER

Seeing the code powering websites you use every day

Understanding the languages used to make websites

Learning how applications are created for mobile devices

Chapter 2

Programming for the Web

To think you can start something in your college dorm room . . . and build something a billion people use is crazy to think about. It's amazing.

—MARK ZUCKERBERG

Programming for the web allows you to reach massive audiences around the world faster than ever before. Four years after its 2004 launch, Facebook had 100 million users, and by 2012 it had over a billion. By contrast, it took desktop software years to reach even 1 million people. These days, mobile phones are increasing the reach of web applications. Although roughly 300 million desktop computers are sold every year, almost 2 billion mobile phones are sold in that time — and the number is steadily increasing.

In this chapter you learn how websites are displayed on your computer or mobile device. I introduce the languages used to program websites, and show you how mobile-device applications are made.

Displaying Web Pages on Your Desktop and Mobile Device

On desktop computers and mobile devices, web pages are displayed by applications called *browsers*. The most popular web browsers include Google Chrome, Mozilla Firefox (formerly Netscape Navigator), Microsoft Internet Explorer, and Apple Safari. Until now, you have likely interacted with websites you visit as an obedient user, and followed the rules the website has created by pointing and clicking when allowed. The first step to becoming a producer and programmer of websites is to peel back the web page, and see and play with the code underneath it all.

Hacking your favorite news website

What's your favorite news website? By following a few steps, you can see and even modify the code used to create that website. (No need to worry, you won't be breaking any rules by following these instructions.)

TIP

Although you can use almost any modern browser to inspect a website's code, these instructions assume you're using the Google Chrome browser. Install the latest version by going to www.google.com/chrome/browser.

To "hack" your favorite news website, follow these steps:

1. **Open your favorite news website using the Chrome browser. (In this example, I use** www.huffingtonpost.com.**)**

2. **Place your mouse cursor over any static fixed headline and right-click once, which opens a contextual menu. Then, left-click once on the Inspect Element menu choice. (See Figure 2-1.)**

TIP

If using a Macintosh computer, you can right-click by holding down the Control key and clicking once.

The Developer Tools panel opens at the bottom of your browser. This panel shows you the code used to create this web page! Highlighted in blue is the specific code used to create the headline where you originally put your mouse cursor. (See Figure 2-2.)

TIP

Look at the left edge of the highlighted code. If you see a right arrow, left-click once on the arrow to expand the code.

FIGURE 2-1:
Right-click on
a headline and
select Inspect
Element from
the menu.

FIGURE 2-2:
The blue high-
lighted code is
used to create
the web page
headline.

3. **Scan the highlighted code carefully for the text of your headline. When you find it, double-click on the headline text. This allows you to edit the headline. (See Figure 2-3.)**

Be careful not to click on anything that begins with http, which is the headline link. Clicking on a headline link will open a new window or tab and load the link.

FIGURE 2-3:
Double-click the headline text to edit it with your own headline.

4. Insert your name in the headline and press Enter.

Your name now appears on the actual web page. (See Figure 2-4.) Enjoy your newfound fame!

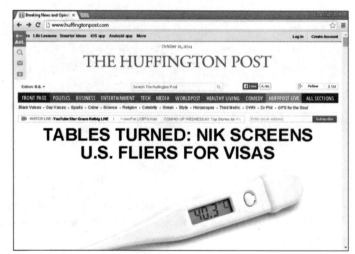

FIGURE 2-4:
You successfully changed the headline of a major news website.

TIP

If you were unable to edit the headline after following these steps, visit http://goggles.webmaker.org for an easier, more guided tutorial. It's a foolproof guided version to edit code on a page. It's a teaching aid that shows that any code on the Internet can be modified. On that page, click the yellow Activate X-Ray Goggles to see and edit the code on the webmaker.org web page. Try again to hack your favorite news website by following the "Remix Any Webpage" instructions.

If you successfully completed the steps above and changed the original headline, it's time for your 15 minutes of fame to come to an end. Reload the web page and the original headline reappears. What just happened? Did your changes appear to everyone visiting the web page? And why did your edited headline disappear?

To answer these questions, you first need to understand how the Internet delivers web pages to your computer.

Understanding how the World Wide Web works

After you type a URL, such as huffingtonpost.com, into your browser, the following steps happen behind the scenes in the seconds before your page loads (see Figure 2-5):

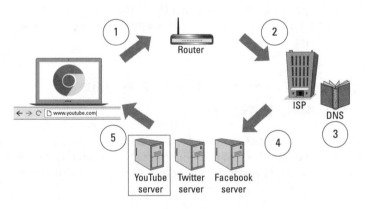

FIGURE 2-5:
Steps followed
to deliver a
website to your
browser.

1. Your computer sends your request for the web page to a router. The router distributes Internet access throughout your home or workplace.

2. The router passes your request onto your Internet service provider (ISP). In the United States, your ISP is a company like Comcast, Time Warner, AT&T, or Verizon.

3. Your ISP then converts the words and characters in your URL— "huffingtonpost. com," in my example—into a numerical address called the *Internet protocol address* (or, more commonly, *IP address*). An IP address is a set of four numbers separated by periods (such as, for example, 192.168.1.1). Just like your physical address, this number is unique, and every computer has one. Your ISP has a digital phone book, similar to a physical phonebook, called a *domain name server* that's used to convert text URLs into IP addresses.

4. With the IP address located, your ISP knows which server on the Internet to forward your request to, and your personal IP address is included in this request.

5. The website server receives your request, and sends a copy of the web page code to your computer for your browser to display.

6. Your web browser renders the code onto the screen.

When you edited the website code using the Developer Tools, you modified only the copy of the website code that exists on your computer, so only you could see the change. When you reloaded the page, you started steps 1 through 6 again, and retrieved a fresh copy of the code from the server, overwriting any changes you made on your computer.

TIP

You may have heard of a software tool called an *ad blocker*. Ad blockers work by editing the local copy of website code, just as you did above, to remove website advertisements. Ad blockers are controversial because websites use advertising revenue to pay for operating costs. If ad blockers continue rising in popularity, ad revenue could dry up, and websites would have to demand that readers pay to see their content.

Watching out for your front end and back end

Now that you know how your browser accesses websites, let us dive deeper into the way the actual website is constructed. As shown in Figure 2-6, the code for websites, and for programs in general, can be divided into four categories, according to the code's function:

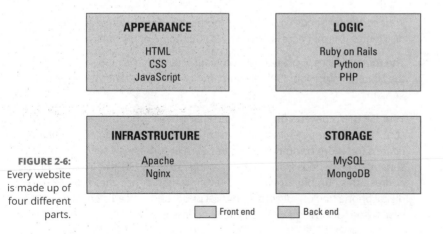

FIGURE 2-6:
Every website is made up of four different parts.

- » **Appearance:** Appearance is the visible part of the website, including content layout and any applied styling, such font size, font typeface, and image size. This category is called the *front end* and is created using languages like HTML, CSS, and JavaScript.

- » **Logic:** Logic determines what content to show and when. For example, a New Yorker accessing a news website should see New York weather, whereas Chicagoans accessing the same site should see Chicago weather. This category is part of the group called the *back end* and is created using languages like Ruby, Python, and PHP. These back end languages can modify the HTML, CSS, and JavaScript that is displayed to the user.

- » **Storage:** Storage saves any data generated by the site and its users. User-generated content, preferences, and profile data must be stored for retrieval later. This category is part of the back end and is stored in databases like MongoDB and MySQL.

- » **Infrastructure:** Infrastructure delivers the website from the server to you, the client machine. When the infrastructure is properly configured, no one notices it, but it can *become* noticeable when a website becomes unavailable due to high traffic from events like presidential elections, the Super Bowl, and natural disasters.

Usually, website developers specialize in one or at most two of these categories. For example, an engineer might really understand the front end and logic languages, or specialize in only databases. Website developers have strengths and specializations, and outside of these areas their expertise is limited, much in the same way that Jerry Seinfeld, a terrific comedy writer, would likely make a terrible romance novelist.

TECHNICAL
STUFF

The rare website developer proficient in all four of these categories is referred to as a *full stack developer.* Usually, smaller companies hire full stack developers, whereas larger companies require the expertise that comes with specialization.

Defining web and mobile applications

Web applications are websites you visit using a web browser on any device. Websites optimized for use on a mobile device, like a phone or tablet, are called *mobile web applications.* By contrast, *native mobile applications* cannot be viewed using a web browser. Instead, native mobile applications are downloaded from an app store like the Apple App Store or Google Play, and designed to run on a specific device such as an iPhone or an Android tablet. Historically, desktop computers outnumbered and outsold mobile devices, but recently two major trends in mobile usage have occurred:

>> In 2014, people with mobile devices outnumbered people with desktop computers. This gap is projected to continue increasing, as shown in Figure 2-7.

>> Mobile-device users spend 80 percent of their time using native mobile applications, and 20 percent of their time browsing mobile websites.

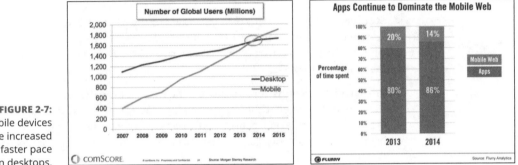

FIGURE 2-7: Mobile devices have increased at a faster pace than desktops.

The increase in mobile devices has happened so quickly over the last 10 years that many companies are becoming "mobile first," designing and developing the mobile version of their applications before the desktop version. WhatsApp and Instagram, two popular mobile applications, first built mobile applications, which continue to have more functionality then their regular websites.

Coding Web Applications

Web applications are easier to build than mobile applications, require little to no additional software to develop and test, and run on all devices, including desktop, laptops, and mobile. Although mobile applications can perform many common web-application tasks, such as email, some tasks are still easier to perform using web applications. For example, booking travel is easier using web applications, especially since the steps necessary — reviewing flights, hotels, and rental cars, and then purchasing all three — are best achieved with multiple windows, access to a calendar, and the entry of substantial personal and payment information.

The programming languages used to code basic web applications, further defined in the following sections, include HTML (Hypertext Markup Language), CSS (Cascading Style Sheets), and JavaScript. Additional features can be added to these websites using languages like Python, Ruby, or PHP.

Starting with HTML, CSS, and JavaScript

Simple websites, such as the one shown in Figure 2-8, are coded using HTML, CSS, and JavaScript. HTML is used to place text on the page, CSS is used to style that text, and JavaScript is used to add interactive effects like the Twitter or Facebook Share button that allows you to share content on social networks and updates the number of other people who have also shared the same content. Websites conveying mainly static, unchanging information are often coded only in these three languages. You will learn about each of these languages in later chapters.

FIGURE 2-8:
The lindaliukas.
fi website, built
using HTML,
CSS, and
JavaScript.

Adding logic with Python, Ruby, or PHP

Websites with more advanced functionality, such as user accounts, file uploads, and e-commerce, typically require a programming language to implement these features. Although Python, Ruby, and PHP are not the only programming languages these sites can use, they are among the most popular. This popularity means there are large online communities of developers who program in these languages, freely post code that you can copy to build common features, and host public online discussions that you can read for solutions to common issues.

Each of these languages also has popular and well documented frameworks. A *framework* is a collection of generic components, such as user accounts and authentication schemes that are reused frequently, allowing developers to build, test, and launch websites more quickly. You can think of a framework as similar to the collection of templates that comes with a word processor. You can design your resume, greeting card, or calendar from scratch, but using the built-in template for each of these document types helps you create your document faster and with greater consistency. Popular frameworks for these languages include

>> Django and Flask for Python

>> Rails and Sinatra for Ruby

>> Zend and Laravel for PHP

Coding Mobile Applications

Mobile applications are hot topics today, in part because mobile apps such as WhatsApp and Instagram were acquired for billions of dollars, and mobile app companies like Rovio, makers of Angry Birds, and King Digital, makers of Candy Crush, generate annual revenues of hundreds of millions to billions of dollars.

When coding mobile applications, developers can either build

>> Mobile web applications, using HTML, CSS, and JavaScript.

>> Native mobile applications using a specific language. For example, Apple devices are programmed using Objective-C or Swift, and Android devices are programmed using Java.

The choice between these two options may seem simple, but there are a few factors at play. Consider the following:

>> Companies developing mobile web applications must make sure the mobile version works across different browsers, different screen sizes, and even different manufacturers, such as Apple, Samsung, RIM, and Microsoft. This results in thousands of possible phone combinations, which can greatly increase the complexity of testing needed before launch. Native mobile apps run only on one phone platform, so there is less variation to account for.

>> Despite running on only one platform, native mobile apps are more expensive and take longer to build than mobile web apps.

>> Some developers have reported that mobile web applications have more performance issues and load more slowly than native mobile applications.

>> As mentioned before, users are spending more time using native mobile applications and less time using browser-based mobile web apps.

>> Native mobile apps are distributed through an app store, which may require approval from the app store owner, whereas mobile web apps are accessible from any web browser. For example, Apple has a strict approval policy and takes up to six days to approve an app for inclusion in the Apple App Store, while Google has a more relaxed approval policy and takes two hours to approve an app.

In one famous example of an app rejected from an app store, Apple blocked Google from launching the Google Voice app in the Apple App Store because it overlapped with Apple's own phone functionality. Google responded by creating a mobile web app accessible from any browser, and Apple could do nothing to block it.

If you're making this choice, consider the complexity of your application. Simple applications, like schedules or menus, can likely be cheaply developed with a mobile web app, whereas more complex applications, like messaging and social networking, may benefit from having a native mobile app. Even well-established technology companies struggle with this choice. Initially, Facebook and LinkedIn created mobile web applications, but both have since shifted to primarily promoting and supporting native mobile apps. The companies cited better speed, memory management, and developer tools as some of the reasons for making the switch.

Building mobile web apps

Although any website can be viewed with a mobile browser, those websites not optimized for mobile devices look a little weird, as if the regular website font size and image dimensions were decreased to fit on a mobile screen. (See Figure 2-9.) By contrast, websites optimized for mobile devices have fonts that are readable, images that scale to the mobile device screen, and a vertical layout suitable for a mobile phone.

Building mobile web apps is done using HTML, CSS, and JavaScript. CSS controls the website appearance across devices based on the screen width. Screens with a small width, such as those on phones, are assigned one vertically-based layout, whereas screens with a larger width, like those on tablets, are assigned another, horizontally-based layout. Because mobile web apps are accessed from the browser, and are not installed on the user's device, these web apps can't send push notifications (alerts) to your phone, run in the background while the browser is minimized, or communicate with other apps.

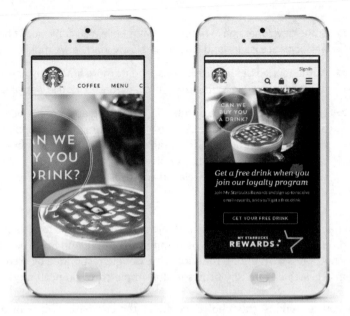

FIGURE 2-9:
Left: starbucks.
com not
optimized for
mobile. Right:
starbucks.com
optimized
for mobile.

Although you can write the HTML, CSS, and JavaScript for your mobile web app from scratch, mobile web frameworks allow you to develop from a base of pre-written code, much like the frameworks for programming languages I mentioned earlier. These mobile web frameworks include a collection of generic components that are reused frequently, and allow developers to build, test, and launch websites more quickly. Twitter Bootstrap is one such mobile web framework, which I introduce in Chapter 8.

Building native mobile apps

Native mobile apps can be faster, more reliable, and look more polished than mobile web apps, as shown in Figure 2-10. Built using Java for use on Android devices, and Objective-C or Swift for use on Apple devices (iOS), native mobile apps must be uploaded to an app store, which may require approvals. The main benefit of an app store is its centralized distribution, and the app may be featured in parts of the app store that can drive downloads. Also, since native mobile applications are programs that are installed on the mobile device, they can be used in more situations without an Internet connection. Finally, and most importantly, users appear to prefer native mobile apps to mobile web apps by a wide margin, one that continues to increase.

Native mobile apps can take advantage of features that run in the background while the app is minimized, such as push notifications, and communicate with other apps, and these features are not available when creating a mobile web app.

FIGURE 2-10:
Left: facebook.com native mobile app. Right: facebook.com mobile web app.

Additionally, native mobile apps perform better when handling graphics-intensive applications, such as games. To be clear, native mobile apps offer better performance and a greater number of features, but they require longer development times and are more expensive to build than mobile web apps.

There is an alternative way to build a native mobile app — a hybrid approach that involves building an app using HTML, CSS, and JavaScript, packaging that code using a "wrapper," and then running the code inside a native mobile app container. The most popular "wrapper" is a product called PhoneGap, and it recognizes specific JavaScript commands that allow access to device-level functionality that's normally inaccessible to mobile web applications. After one version of the app is built, native mobile app containers can be launched for up to nine platforms including Apple, Android, Blackberry, and Windows Phone. The major advantage to using this hybrid approach is building your app once, and then releasing it to so many platforms simultaneously.

TIP

Imagine you knew how to play the piano, but you wanted to also learn how to play the violin. One way you could do this is to buy a violin and start learning how to play. Another option is to buy a synthesizer keyboard, set the tone to violin, and play the keyboard to sound like a violin. This is similar to the hybrid approach, except, in this example, the piano is HTML, CSS, and JavaScript, the violin is a native iOS app, and the synthesizer keyboard is a wrapper like PhoneGap. Just like the synthesizer keyboard can be set to violin, cello, or guitar, so too can PhoneGap create native apps for Apple, Android, and other platforms.

WHAT ABOUT ALL THOSE OTHER PROGRAMMING LANGUAGES? (C, JAVA, AND SO ON)

You may wonder why so many languages exist, and what they all do. Programming languages are created when a developer sees a need not addressed by the current languages. For example, Apple recently created the Swift programming language to make developing iPhone and iPad apps easier than Objective-C, the current programming language used. After they're created, programming languages are very similar to spoken languages, like English or Latin. If developers code using the new language, then it thrives and grows in popularity, like English has over the last six centuries; otherwise, the programming language suffers the same fate as Latin, and becomes a dead language.

You may remember languages like C++, Java, and FORTRAN. These languages still exist today, and they're used in more places than you might think. C++ is preferred when speed and performance is extremely important, and is used to program web browsers, such as Chrome, Firefox, and Safari, along with games like Call of Duty, and Counter Strike. Java is preferred by many large-scale business, and is also the language used to program apps for the Android phone. Finally, FORTRAN is not as widespread or popular as it once was, but it is popular within the scientific community, and it powers some functionality in the financial sector, especially at some of the largest banks in the world, many of which continue to have old code.

As long as programmers think of faster and better ways to program, new programming languages will continue to be created, while older languages fall out of favor.

Chapter 3

Becoming a Programmer

The way to get started is to quit talking and begin doing.

— WALT DISNEY

P rogramming is a skill that can be learned by anyone. You might be a student in college wondering how to start learning, or a professional hoping to find a new job or improve your performance at your current job. In just about every case, the best way to learn how to code is to

>> Have a goal of what you would like to build.

>> Actually start coding.

In this chapter, you discover the process every programmer follows when programming, and the different roles programmers play to create a program (or, more commonly these days, an "app"). You also learn the tools to use when coding either offline or online.

Writing Code Using a Process

Writing code is much like painting, furniture making, or cooking — it isn't always obvious how the end product was created. However, all programs, even mysterious ones, are created using a process. Two of the most popular processes used today are

>> **Waterfall:** A set of *sequential* steps followed to create a program.

>> **Agile:** A set of *iterative* steps followed to create a program. (See Figure 3-1.)

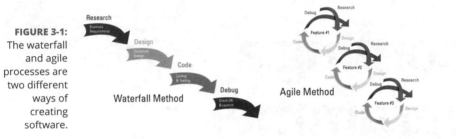

FIGURE 3-1:
The waterfall and agile processes are two different ways of creating software.

Let me describe a specific scenario to explain how these two process work. Imagine you want to build a restaurant app that does the following two things:

>> It displays restaurant information, such as the hours of operation and the menu.

>> It allows users to make or cancel reservations.

Using the waterfall method, you'd define everything the app needs to do: You'd design both the information-display and the reservation parts of the app, code the entire app, and then release the app to users. By contrast, using the agile method, you would define, design, and code only the information-display portion of the app, release it to users, and collect feedback. Based on the feedback collected, you would then redesign and make changes to the information-display to address major concerns. When you were satisfied with the information-display piece, you'd then define, design, and build the reservation part of the app. Again, you would collect feedback and refine the reservation feature to address major concerns.

The agile methodology stresses shorter development times, and has increased in popularity as the pace of technological change has increased. The waterfall approach, on the other hand, demands that the developer code and release the entire app at once, but since completing a large project takes an enormous amount of time, changes in technology may have occurred before the finished product arrives. If you used the waterfall method to create our restaurant-app example, the technology to take user reservations may have changed by the time you get around to coding that portion of the app. Still, the waterfall approach remains popular in certain contexts, such as with financial and government software, where requirements and approval are obtained at the beginning of a project, and whose documentation of a project must be complete.

TECHNICAL STUFF

The healthcare.gov website, released in October 2013, was developed using a waterfall style process. Testing of all the code occurred in September 2013, when the entire system was assembled. Unfortunately, the tests occurred too late and were not comprehensive, resulting in not enough time to fix errors before launching the site publicly.

Regardless of whether you pick the agile or waterfall methodology, coding an app involves four steps:

1. Researching what you want to build

2. Designing your app

3. Coding your app

4. Debugging your code

REMEMBER

On average, you will spend much more time researching, designing, and debugging your app than doing the actual coding, which is the opposite of what you may expect.

These steps are described in the sections that follow. You'll use this process when you create your own app in Chapter 10.

Researching what you want to build

You have an idea for a web or mobile application, and usually it starts with "Wouldn't it be great if. . ." Before writing any code, it helps to do some investigating. Consider the possibilities in your project as you answer the following questions:

>> What similar website/app already exists? What technology was used to build it?

>> Which features should I include—and more importantly exclude—in my app?

>> Which providers can help create these features? For example, companies like Google, Yahoo, Microsoft, or others may have software already built that you could incorporate into your app.

To illustrate, consider the restaurant app I discussed earlier. When conducting market research and answering the three questions above, searching using Google is usually the best resource. Searching for *restaurant reservation app* shows existing restaurant apps that include OpenTable, SeatMe, and Livebookings. OpenTable, for example, allows users to reserve a table from restaurants displayed on a map using Google Maps.

In the restaurant app example, you'd want to research exactly what kinds of restaurant information you'd need to provide, and how extensive the reservation system portion of the app should be. In addition, for each of these questions you must decide whether to build the feature from scratch or use an existing provider. For example, when providing restaurant information do you want to just show name, cuisine, address, telephone number, and hours of operation, or do you also want to show restaurant menus? When showing restaurant data, do you prefer extensive coverage of a single geographical area, or do you want national coverage even if that means you'd cover fewer restaurants in any specific area?

Designing your app

Your app's visual design incorporates all of your research and describes exactly how your users will interact with every page and feature. Because your users will be accessing your site from desktop, laptop, and mobile devices, you'd want to make sure you create a responsive (multi-device) design and carefully consider how your site will look on all these devices. At this stage of the process, a general web designer, illustrator, or user interface specialist will help create visual designs for the app.

TIP

Many responsive app designs and templates can be found on the Internet and used freely. For specific examples, see Chapter 8, or search Google using the query *responsive website design examples*.

There are two types of visual designs (see Figure 3-2):

>> **Wireframes:** These are low fidelity website drawings that show structurally the ways your content and your site's interface interact.

>> **Mockups:** These are high fidelity website previews that include colors, images, and logos.

TIP

Balsamiq is a popular tool used to create wireframes, and Photoshop is a popular tool to create mockups. However, you can avoid paying for additional software by using PowerPoint (PC), Keynote (Mac), or the free and open-source OpenOffice to create your app designs.

TECHNICAL
STUFF

Professional designers create mockups with Adobe Photoshop and use *layers*, which isolate individual site elements. A properly created layered Photoshop file helps developers more easily write the code for those website elements.

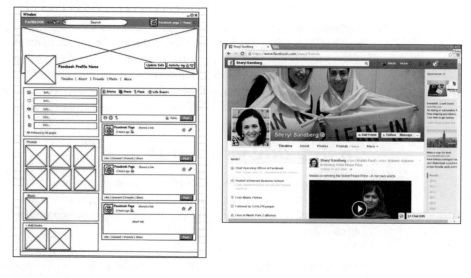

FIGURE 3-2:
Wireframes
(left) are simple
site renderings,
whereas
mockups
(right) show full
site previews.

In addition to visual design, complex apps will also have technical designs and decisions to finalize. For example, if your app stores and retrieves user data you will need a database to perform these tasks. Initial decisions here will include the type of database to add, the specific database provider to use, and the best way to integrate the database into the application. Additionally, developers must design the database by choosing the fields to store. The process is similar to the process of creating a spreadsheet to model a company's income — you first decide the number of columns to use, and whether you'll include fields as a percentage of revenue or a numerical value, and so on. Similarly, other features like user logins or credit card payments all require you to make choices on how to implement these features.

Coding your app

With research and design done, you are now ready to code your application. In everyday web development, you would begin by choosing which pages and features to start coding. As you work through the projects in this book, however, I will guide you on what to code first.

Knowing how much to code and when to stop can be tough. Developers call the first iteration of an app the *minimum viable product* — meaning you've coded just enough to test your app with real users and receive feedback. If no one likes your app or thinks it's useful, it's best to find out as soon as possible.

An app is the sum of its features, and for any individual feature it's a good idea to write the minimum code necessary and then add to it. For example, your restaurant app may have a toolbar at the top of the page with drop-down menus. Instead of trying to create the whole menu at once, it's better to just create the menu, and then later create the drop-down menu effect.

Projects can involve front-end developers, who'll code the appearance of the app, and back-end developers, who'll code the logic and create databases. A "full stack developer" is one who can do both front-end and back-end development. On large projects it's more common to see specialized front-end and back-end developers, along with project managers who ensure everyone is communicating with each other and adhering to the schedule so the project finishes on time.

Debugging your code

Debugging is going to be a natural part of any application. The computer always follows your instructions exactly and yet no program ever works as you expect it to. Debugging can be frustrating. Three of the more common mistakes to watch out for are

>> **Syntax errors:** These are errors caused by misspelling words/commands, by omitting characters, or by including extra characters. Some languages, such as HTML and CSS, are forgiving of these errors and your code will still work even with some syntax errors, whereas other languages, such as JavaScript, are more particular and your code won't run when any such error is present.

>> **Logic errors:** These are harder to fix. With logic errors, your syntax is correct but the program behaves differently than you expected, such as when the prices of the items in the shopping cart of an e-commerce site do not sum up to the correct total.

>> **Display errors:** These are common mainly to web applications. With display errors, your program might run and work properly, but it won't appear properly. Web apps today run on many devices, browsers, and screen sizes, so extensive testing is the only way to catch these types of errors.

TECHNICAL STUFF

The word *debugging* was popularized in the 1940s by Grace Hopper, who fixed a computer error by literally removing a moth from a computer.

Picking Tools for the Job

Now you're ready to actually start coding. You can develop websites either offline, by working with an editor, or online, with a web service such as Codecademy.com. Especially if you have never done any coding before, I would strongly recommend you code with access to an Internet connection using the Codecademy.com platform because you do not have to download and install any software to start coding, you do not have to find a web host to serve your web pages, and you do not need to upload your web page to a web host. As you code, the Codecademy.com platform will do these tasks for you automatically.

Working offline

To code offline, you'll need the following:

>> **Editor:** This refers to the text editor you'll use to write all the code you learn in this book, including HTML, CSS, JavaScript, Ruby, Python, and PHP. The editor you use will depend on the type of computer you have:

- *PC:* Use the pre-installed Notepad, or install Notepad++, a free editor available for download at http://notepad-plus-plus.org.

- *Mac:* Use the pre-installed TextEdit or install TextMate 2.0, an open-source editor available for download at http://macromates.com.

>> **Browser:** Many browsers exist, including Firefox, Safari, Internet Explorer, and Opera; however, I recommend you use Chrome, because it offers the most support for the latest HTML standards. It's available for download at www.google.com/chrome/browser.

>> **Web host:** In order for your website code to be accessible to everyone on the Internet, you need to host your website online. Freemium web hosts include Weebly (www.weebly.com) and Wix (www.wix.com); these sites offer basic hosting but charge for additional features like additional storage or removing ads. Google provides free web hosting through Sites (http://sites.google.com) and Drive (http://drive.google.com).

Working online with Codecademy.com

Codecademy.com is the easiest way to start learning how to code online, and lessons from the site form the basis of this book. The site doesn't require you to install a code editor or sign up for a web host before you start coding, and it's free to individual users like you.

The site can be accessed using any up-to-date modern browser, but Google Chrome or Mozilla Firefox is recommended.

Touring the learning environment

After signing up or signing into the site, you will either see an interactive card or the coding interface, depending on the content you learn. (See Figure 3-3.)

The interactive cards allow you to click toggle buttons to demonstrate effects of pre-written code, whereas the coding interface has an coding editor and a live preview window that shows you the effects of the code entered into the coding editor.

FIGURE 3-3:
Codecademy.
com interac-
tive cards (left)
and the coding
interface
(right).

The coding interface has four parts:

» Background information on the upper-left side of the screen tells you about the coding task you are about to do.

» The lower-left side of the screen shows instructions to complete in the coding window.

» The coding window allows you to follow the exercise instructions and write code. The coding window also includes a preview screen that shows a live preview of your code as you type.

» After completing the coding instructions, press Save & Submit or Run. If you successfully followed the instructions, you advance to the next exercise; otherwise, the site will give you a helpful error message and a hint.

The interactive cards have three parts:

» Background information about a coding concept.

» A coding window to complete one simple coding task. A preview window also shows a live preview of your code as you type.

» After completing the coding instructions, press the Got It button. You can review any previous interactive cards by clicking the Go Back button.

Receiving support from the community

If you run into a problem or have a bug you cannot fix, try the following steps:

» Click on the hint underneath the instructions.

» Use the Q&A Forums to post your problem or question, and review questions others have posted.

» Tweet me at @nikhilgabraham with your question or problem, and include the hashtag #codingFD at the end of your tweet.

2

Building the Silent and Interactive Web Page

Chapter 4
Exploring Basic HTML

You affect the world by what you browse.

— TIM BERNERS-LEE

HTML, or *HyperText Markup Language*, is used in every single web page you browse on the Internet. Because the language is so foundational, a good first step for you is to start learning HTML.

In this chapter, you learn HTML basics, including basic HTML structure and how to make text appear in the browser. Next, you learn how to format text and display images in a web browser. Finally, you create your own, and possibly first, HTML website. You may find that HTML without any additional styling appears to be very plain, and does not look like the websites you normally visit on the Internet. After you code a basic website using HTML, you will use additional languages in later chapters to add even more style to your websites.

What Does HTML Do?

HTML instructs the browser on how to display text and images in a web page. Recall the last time you created a document with a word processor. Whether you use Microsoft Word or Wordpad, Apple Pages, or another application, your word processor has a main window in which you type text, and a menu or toolbar with multiple options to structure and style that text (see Figure 4-1). Using your word processor, you can create headings, write in paragraphs, insert pictures, or underline text. Similarly, you can use HTML to structure and style text that appears on websites.

Markup language documents, like HTML documents, are just plain text files. Unlike documents created with a word processor, you can view an HTML file using any web browser on any type of computer.

HTML files are plain text files that will appear styled only when viewed with a browser. By contrast, the rich text file format used by word processors add unseen formatting commands to the file. As a result, HTML written in a rich text file won't render correctly in the browser.

REMEMBER

Understanding HTML Structure

HTML follows a few rules to ensure that a website will always display in the same way no matter which browser or computer is used. Once you understand these rules, you'll be better able to predict how the browser will display your HTML pages, and to diagnose your mistakes when (not if!) the browser displays your web page differently than you expected. Since its creation, HTML has evolved to include more effects, but the following basic structural elements remain unchanged.

You can use any browser to display your HTML files, though I strongly recommend you download, install, and use Chrome or Firefox. Both of these browsers are updated often, are generally fast, and support and consistently render the widest variety of HTML tags.

TIP

Identifying elements

HTML uses special text keywords called *elements* to structure and style a website. The browser recognizes an element and applies its effect if the following three conditions exist:

>> The element is a letter, word, or phrase with special meaning. For example, h1 is an element recognized by the browser to apply a header effect, with bold text and an enlarged font size.

>> The element is enclosed with a left-angle bracket (<) and right-angle bracket (>). An element enclosed in this way is called a *tag* (such as, for example, <h1>).

>> An opening tag (<element>) is followed by a closing tag (</element>). Note that the closing tag differs from the opening tag by the addition of a forward slash after the first left bracket and before the element (such as, for example, </h1>).

REMEMBER

Some HTML tags are self-closing, and don't need separate closing tags, only a forward slash in the opening tag. For more about this, see the section, "Getting Familiar with Common HTML Tasks and Tags," later in this chapter.

When all three conditions are met, the text between the opening and closing tags is styled with the tag's defined effect. If even one of these conditions is not met, the browser just displays plain text.

For a better understanding of these three conditions, see the example code below:

```
<h1>This is a big heading with all three conditions</h1>
h1 This is text without the < and > sign surrounding the tag /h1
<rockstar>This is text with a tag that has no meaning to the browser</rockstar>
This is regular text
```

You can see how a browser would display this code in Figure 4-2.

FIGURE 4-2:
The example code displayed in a browser.

The browser applies a header effect to "This is a big heading with all three conditions" because h1 is a header tag and all three conditions for a valid HTML tag exist:

>> The browser recognizes the h1 element.

>> The h1 element is surrounded with a left (<) and right angle bracket (>).

>> The opening tag (<h1>) is followed by text and then a closing tag (</h1>).

TIP

Notice how the h1 tag itself does not display in the heading. The browser will never display the actual text of an element in a properly formatted HTML tag.

The remaining lines of code display as plain text because they each are missing one of the conditions. On the second line of code, the <h1> tag is missing the left and right brackets, which violates the second condition. The third line of code violates the first condition because rockstar is not a recognized HTML element. (Once you finish this chapter, however, you may feel like a rockstar!) Finally, the fourth line of code displays as plain text because it has no opening tag preceding the text, and no closing tag following the text, which violates the third condition.

REMEMBER

Every left angle-bracket must be followed after the element with a right angle-bracket. In addition, every opening HTML tag must be followed with a closing HTML tag.

Over 100 HTML elements exist, and we cover the most important elements in the following sections. For now, don't worry about memorizing individual element names.

WARNING

HTML is a forgiving language, and may properly apply an effect even if you're missing pieces of code, like a closing tag. However, if you leave in too many errors, your page won't display correctly.

Featuring your best attribute

Attributes provide additional ways to modify the behavior of an element or specify additional information. Usually, but not always, you set an attribute equal to a value enclosed in quotes. Here's an example using the title attribute and the hidden attribute:

```
<h1 title="United States of America">USA</h1>
<h1 hidden>New York City</h1>
```

The title attribute provides advisory information about the element that appears when the mouse cursor hovers over the affected text (in other words, a *tooltip*). In this example, the word USA is styled as a header using the <h1> tag with a title attribute set equal to "United States of America". In a browser, then, when you place your mouse cursor over the word USA, the text United States of America displays as a tooltip. (See Figure 4-3.)

FIGURE 4-3:
A heading with title attribute has a tooltip.

The hidden attribute indicates that the element is not relevant, so the browser won't render any elements with this attribute. In this example, the words New York City never appear in the browser window because the hidden attribute is in the opening <h1> tag. More practically, hidden attributes are often used to hide fields from users so they can't edit them. For example, an RSVP website may want to include but hide from user view a date and time field.

TECHNICAL STUFF

The hidden attribute is new in HTML5, which means it may not work on some older browsers.

You don't have to use one attribute at a time. You can include multiple attributes in the opening HTML tag, like this:

```
<h1 title="United States of America" lang="en">USA</h1>
```

In this example, I used the title attribute, and the lang attribute, setting it equal to "en" to specify that the content of the element is in the English language.

REMEMBER

When including multiple attributes, separate each attribute with one space.

Keep the following rules in mind when using attributes:

>> If using an attribute, always include the attribute in the opening HTML tag.

>> Multiple attributes can modify a single element.

>> If the attribute has a value, then use the equal sign (=) and enclose the value in quotes.

Standing head, title, and body above the rest

HTML files are structured in a specific way so browsers can correctly interpret the file's information. Every HTML file has the same five elements: four whose opening and closing tags appear once and only once, and one that appears once and doesn't need a closing tag. These are as follows:

TECHNICAL STUFF

» !DOCTYPE html must appear first in your HTML file, and it appears only once. This tag lets browsers know which version of HTML you are using. In this case, it's the latest version, HTML5. No closing tag is necessary for this element.

For HTML4 websites, the first line in the HTML file would read < !DOCTYPE HTML PUBLIC "-//W3C//DTD HTML 4.01//EN" "http://www.w3.org/TR/html4/strict.dtd">

» html represents the *root* or beginning of an HTML document. The <html> tag is followed by first an opening and closing <head> tag, and then an opening and closing <body> tag.

» head contains other elements, which specify general information about the page, including the title.

» title defines the title in the browser's title bar or page tab. Search engines like Google use title to rank websites in search results.

» body contains the main content of an HTML document. Text, images, and other content listed between the opening and closing body tag is displayed by the browser.

Here is an example of a properly structured HTML file with these five tags (see Figure 4-4):

```
<!DOCTYPE html>
<html>
<head>
    <title>Favorite Movie Quotes</title>
</head>
<body>
    <h1>"I'm going to make him an offer he can't refuse"</h1>
    <h1>"Houston, we have a problem"</h1>
    <h1>"May the Force be with you"</h1>
    <h1>"You talking to me?"</h1>
</body>
</html>
```

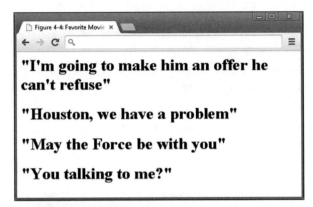

FIGURE 4-4:
A web page created with basic HTML elements.

TIP

Using spaces to indent and separate your tags is highly recommended. It helps you and others read and understand your code. These spaces are only for you and any other human that reads the code, however. Your browser won't care. As far as your browser is concerned, you could run all your tags together on one line. (Don't do this, though. The next person that reads your code will be most unhappy.) HTML does recognize and display the first whitespace character in text between opening and closing HTML tags.

REMEMBER

Our example had many h1 tags but only one opening and closing `html`, `head`, `title`, and `body` tag.

Getting Familiar with Common HTML Tasks and Tags

Your browser can interpret over a hundred HTML tags, but most websites use just a few tags to do most of the work within the browser. To understand this, let's try a little exercise: Think of your favorite news website. Have one in mind? Now connect to the Internet, open your browser, and type in the address of that website. Bring this book with you, and take your time — I can wait!

In the event you can't access the Internet right now, take a look at the article from my favorite news website, *The New York Times,* found in Figure 4-5.

Look closely at the news website on your screen (or look at mine). Four HTML elements are used to create the majority of the page:

>> **Headlines:** Headlines are displayed in bold and have a larger font size than the surrounding text.

>> **Paragraphs:** Each story is organized into paragraphs with white space dividing each paragraph.

>> **Hyperlinks:** The site's homepage and article pages have links to other stories, and links to share the story on social networks like Facebook, Twitter, and Google+.

>> **Images:** Writers place images throughout the story, but also look for site images like icons and logos.

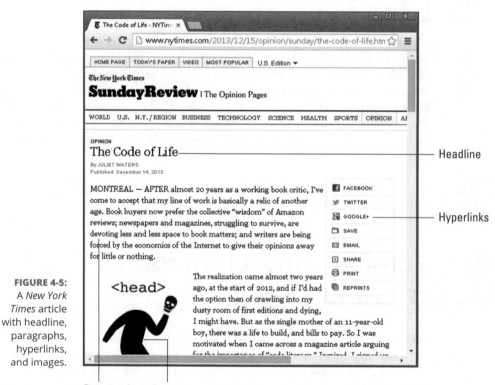

FIGURE 4-5:
A *New York Times* article with headline, paragraphs, hyperlinks, and images.

In the following sections I explain how to write code to create these common HTML features.

Writing headlines

Use headlines to describe a section of your page. HTML has six levels of headings (see Figure 4-6):

>> h1, which is used for the most important headings

>> h2, which is used for subheadings

>> h3 to h6, which are used for less important headings

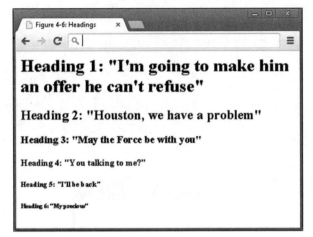

FIGURE 4-6:
Headings
created using
elements h1
through h6.

The browser renders h1 headings with a font size larger than h2's, which in turn is larger than h3's. Headings start with an opening heading tag, the heading text, and then the closing heading tag, as follows:

```
<h1>Heading text here</h1>
```

Here are some additional code examples showing various headings:

```
<h1>Heading 1: "I'm going to make him an offer he can't refuse"</h1>
<h2>Heading 2: "Houston, we have a problem"</h2>
<h3>Heading 3: "May the Force be with you"</h3>
<h4>Heading 4: "You talking to me?"</h4>
<h5>Heading 5: "I'll be back"</h5>
<h6>Heading 6: "My precious"</h6>
```

REMEMBER

Always close what you open. With headings, remember to include a closing heading tag, such as </h1>.

Organizing text in paragraphs

To display text in paragraphs you can use the p element: Place an opening <p> tag before the paragraph, and a closing tag after it. The p element takes text and inserts a line break after the closing tag.

To insert a single line break after any element, use the ⟨br⟩ tag. The ⟨br⟩ tag is self-closing so no closing tag is needed, and ⟨/br⟩ is not used.

Paragraphs start with an opening paragraph tag, the paragraph text, and then the closing paragraph tag:

```
<p>Paragraph text here</p>
```

Some additional examples of coding a paragraph (see Figure 4-7):

```
<p>Armstrong: Okay. I'm going to step off the LM now.</p>
<p>Armstrong: That's one small step for man; one giant leap for mankind.</p>
<p>Armstrong: Yes, the surface is fine and powdery. I can kick it up loosely with my toe.
             It does adhere in fine layers, like powdered charcoal, to the sole and sides
             of my boots.</p>
```

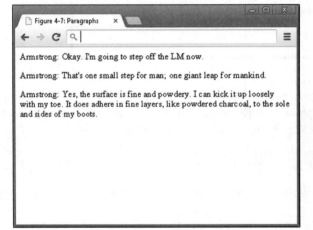

FIGURE 4-7:
Text displayed in paragraphs using the p element.

Linking to your (heart's) content

Hyperlinks are one of HTML's most valuable features. Web pages that include hyperlinked references to other sources allow the reader to access those sources with just a click, a big advantage over printed pages.

Hyperlinks have two parts:

>> **Link destination:** The web page the browser visits once the link is clicked.

To define the link destination in HTML, start with an opening anchor tag (⟨a⟩) that has an href attribute. Then, add the value of the href attribute, which is the website the browser will go to once the link is clicked.

>> **Link description:** The words used to describe the link.

To do this, add text to describe the link after the opening anchor tag, and then add the closing anchor tag.

The resulting HTML should look something like this:

```
<a href="website url">Link description</a>
```

Three more examples of coding a hyperlink (see Figure 4-8):

```
<a href="http://www.amazon.com">Purchase anything</a>
<a href="http://www.airbnb.com">Rent a place to stay from a local host</a>
<a href="http://www.techcrunch.com">Tech industry blog</a>
```

FIGURE 4-8:
Three hyperlinks created using the a element.

When rendering hyperlinks, the browser, by default, will underline the link and color the link blue. To change these default properties, see Chapter 6.

The `<a>` tag does not include a line break after the link.

REMEMBER

TECHNICAL STUFF

Google's search engine ranks web pages based on the words used to describe a web page between the opening and closing `<a>` tags. This improved on search results from previous methods, which relied primarily on analyzing page content.

Adding images

Images spruce up otherwise plain HTML text pages. To include an image on your web page — your own or someone else's — you must obtain the image's web address. Websites like Google Images (images.google.com) and Flickr (www.flickr.com) allow you to search for online images based on keywords. When you find an image you like, right-click on the image, and select Copy Image URL.

WARNING

Make sure you have permission to use an online image. Flickr has tools that allow you to search for images with few to no license restrictions. Additionally, websites pay to host images, and incur charges when a website directly links to an image. For this reason, some websites do not allow *hotlinking*, or linking directly from third-party websites (like you) to an image.

TIP

If you want to use an image that has not already been uploaded to the Internet, you can use a site like www.imgur.com to upload the image. After uploading, you will be able to copy the image URL and use it in your HTML.

To include an image, start with an opening image tag `<img>`, define the source of the image using the `src` attribute, and include a forward slash at the end of the opening tag to close the tag (see Figure 4-9):

```
<img src="http://upload.wikimedia.org/wikipedia/commons/5/55/Grace_Hopper.jpg"/>
<img src="http://upload.wikimedia.org/wikipedia/commons/b/bd/ Dts_news_bill_gates_
    wikipedia.JPG"/>
```

FIGURE 4-9:
Images of Grace Hopper, a US Navy rear admiral, and Bill Gates, the co-founder of Microsoft, rendered using `<img>`.

TIP

The image tag is self-closing, which means a separate `</img>` closing image tag is not used. The image tag is one of the exceptions to the always-close-what-you-open rule!

Styling Me Pretty

Now that you know how to display basic text and images in a browser, you should understand how to further customize and style them. HTML has basic capabilities to style content, and later chapters show you how to use CSS to style and position your content down to the last pixel. Here, however, I explain how to do some basic text formatting in HTML, and then you'll build your first web page.

Highlighting with bold, italics, underline, and strikethrough

HTML allows for basic text styling using the following elements:

>> strong marks important text, which the browser displays as bold.

>> em marks emphasized text, which the browser displays as italicized.

>> u marks text as underlined.

>> del marks deleted text, which the browser displays as strikethrough.

REMEMBER

The underline element is not typically used for text because it can lead to confusion. Hyperlinks, after all, are underlined by default.

To use these elements, start with the element's opening tag, followed by the affected text, and then a closing tag, as follows:

```
<element name>Affected text</element name>
```

Some examples (see Figure 4-10):

```
Grace Hopper, <strong> a US Navy rear admiral </strong>, popularized the term "debugging."
Bill Gates co-founded a company called <em>Microsoft</em>.
Stuart Russell and Peter Norvig wrote a book called <u>Artificial Intelligence: A Modern
    Approach</u>.
Mark Zuckerberg created a website called <del>Nosebook</del> Facebook.
Steve Jobs co-founded a company called <del><em>Peach</em></del> <em>Apple</em>
```

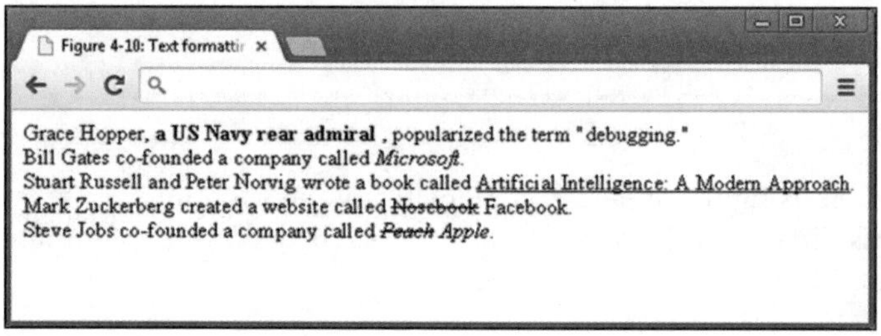

FIGURE 4-10:
Sentences formatted using bold, italics, underline, and strikethrough.

> Figure 4-10: Text formattir ×
>
> Grace Hopper, **a US Navy rear admiral** , popularized the term "debugging."
> Bill Gates co-founded a company called *Microsoft*.
> Stuart Russell and Peter Norvig wrote a book called <u>Artificial Intelligence: A Modern Approach</u>.
> Mark Zuckerberg created a website called ~~Nosebook~~ Facebook.
> Steve Jobs co-founded a company called ~~*Peach*~~ *Apple*.

TIP

You can apply multiple effects to text by using multiple HTML tags. Always close the most recently opened tag first and then the next most recently used tag. For an example, look at the last line of code in Figure 4-10, and the tags applied to the word Peach.

Raising and lowering text with superscript and subscript

Reference works like *Wikipedia*, and technical papers often use superscript for foot-notes and subscript for chemical names. To apply these styles, use the elements

» sub for text marked as superscript

» sub for text marked as subscript

To use these elements, start with the element's opening tag, followed by the affected text, and then a closing tag as follows:

```
<element name>Affected text</element name>
```

Two examples (see Figure 4-11):

```
<p>The University of Pennsylvania announced to the public the first electronic general-
    purpose computer, named ENIAC, on February 14, 1946.<sup>1</sup></p>
<p>The Centers for Disease Control and Prevention recommends drinking several glasses of
    H<sub>2</sub>0 per day.</p>
```

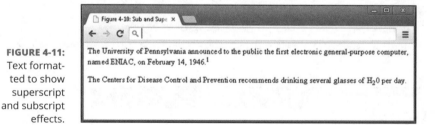

FIGURE 4-11: Text format-ted to show superscript and subscript effects.

TIP

When using the superscript element to mark footnotes, use an `<a>` anchor tag to link directly to the footnote so the reader can view the footnote easily.

Building Your First Website Using HTML

Now that you have learned the basics, you can put that knowledge to use. You can practice directly on your computer by following these steps:

1. **Open any text editor, such as Notepad (on a PC) or TextEdit (on a Mac).**

On a PC running Microsoft Windows, you can access Notepad by clicking the Start button and selecting Run; in the search box, type *Notepad*. On a Macintosh, select the Spotlight Search (hourglass icon on the top-right corner of the toolbar), and type *TextEdit*.

2. **Enter into the text editor any of the code samples you have seen in this chapter, or create your own combination of the code.**

3. **Once you have finished, save the file and make sure to include ".html" at the end of the filename.**

4. **Double-click on the file, which should open in your default browser.**

TIP

You can download at no cost specialized text editors that have been created specifically for writing code. For PCs, you can download Notepad++ at www.notepad-plus-plus.org. For Mac computers, you can download TextMate at http://macromates.com/download.

If you would like to practice your HTML online, you can use the Codecademy website. Codecademy is a free website created in 2011 to allow anyone to learn how to code right in the browser, without installing or downloading any software. (See Figure 4-12.) Practice all of the tags (and a few more) that you learned in this chapter by following these steps:

1. **Open your browser, go to** www.dummies.com/go/coding, **and click on the Codecademy link.**

2. **Sign up for a Codecademy account or sign in if you already have an account. Creating an account allows you to save your progress as you work, but it's optional.**

3. **Navigate to and click on HTML Basics.**

4. **Background information is presented in the upper-left portion of the site, and instructions are presented in the lower-left portion of the site.**

5. **Complete the instructions in the main coding window. As you type, a live preview of your code is generated.**

6. **After you have finished completing the instructions, click the Save and Submit Code button.**

If you have followed the instructions correctly, a green checkmark appears, and you proceed to the next exercise. If an error exists in your code a warning appears with a suggested fix. If you run into a problem, or have a bug you cannot fix, click on the hint, use the Q&A Forums, or tweet me at @nikhilga–braham and include hashtag #codingFD.

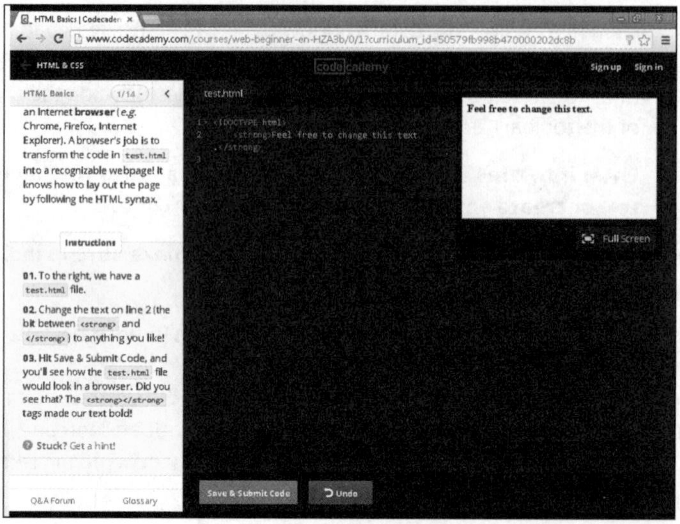

FIGURE 4-12:
Codecademy in-browser exercises.

HISTORY OF HTML

A computer engineer, Tim Berners-Lee, wanted academics to easily access academic papers and collaborate with each other. To accomplish this goal, in 1989 Mr. Berners-Lee created the first version of HTML, which had the same hyperlink elements you learned in this chapter, and hosted the first website in 1991. Unlike most other computer software, Mr. Berners-Lee made HTML available royalty-free, allowing widespread adoption and use around the world. Shortly after creating the first iteration of HTML, Mr. Berners-Lee formed the W3C ("World Wide Web Consortium"), which is a group of people from academic institutions and corporations who define and maintain the HTML language. The W3C continues to develop the HTML language, and has defined more than 100 HTML elements, far more than the 18 Mr. Berners-Lee originally created. The latest version of HTML is HTML5, and it has considerable new functionality. In addition to supporting elements from previous HTML versions, HTML5 allows browsers to play audio and video files, easily locate a user's physical location, and build charts and graphs.

Chapter 5

Getting More Out of HTML

I'm controlling, and I want everything orderly, and I need lists.

— SANDRA BULLOCK

Even your best content needs structure to increase readability for your users. This book is no exception. Consider the "In This Chapter" bulleted list of items at the top of this page, or the table of contents at the beginning of the book. Lists and tables make things easier for you to understand at a glance. By mirroring the structure you find in a book or magazine, web elements let you precisely define how content, such as text and images, appear on the web.

In this chapter, you learn how to use HTML elements such as lists, tables, and forms, and how to know when these elements are appropriate for your content.

Organizing Content on the Page

Readability is the most important principle for organizing and displaying content on your web page. Your web page should allow visitors to easily read, understand, and act on your content. The desired action you have in mind for your visitors may be to click on and read additional content, share the content with others, or perhaps make a purchase. Poorly organized content will lead users to leave your website before engaging with your content for long enough to complete the desired action.

Figures 5-1 and 5-2 show two examples of website readability. In Figure 5-1, I searched Craigslist.org for an apartment in New York. The search results are structured like a list, and you can limit the content displayed using the filters and search forms. Each listing has multiple attributes, such as a description, the number of bedrooms, the neighborhood, and, most importantly, the price. Comparing similar attributes from different listings takes some effort — notice the jagged line your eye must follow.

FIGURE 5-1: A Craigslist.org listing of apartments in New York (2014).

Figure 5-2 shows the results of a search I conducted at Hipmunk.com for flights from New York to London. As with the Craigslist search results, you can limit the content displayed using the filters and search forms. Additionally, each flight listing has multiple attributes, including price, carrier, departure time, landing time, and duration, which are similar to the attributes of the apartment listings. Comparing similar attributes from different flights is much easier with the Hipmunk layout, however. Notice how the content, in contrast to Craigslist's, has a layout that allows your eye to follow a straight line down the page, so you can easily rank and compare different options.

TIP

Don't underestimate the power of simplicity when displaying content. Although Craigslist's content layout may look almost too simple, the site is one of the top 50 most visited websites in the world. Reddit.com is another example of a top 50 website with a simple layout.

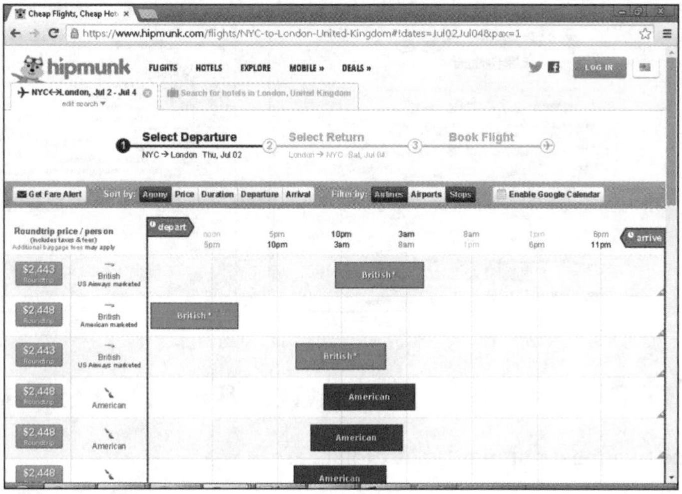

FIGURE 5-2:
A Hipmunk.
com listing of
flights from
New York to
London (2014).

Before displaying your content, ask yourself a few questions first:

>> **Does your content have one attribute with related data, or does it follow sequential steps?** If so, consider using lists.

>> **Does your content have multiple attributes suitable for comparison?** If so, consider using tables.

>> **Do you need to collect input from the visitor?** If so, consider using forms.

TIP

Don't let these choices overwhelm you. Pick one, see how your visitors react, and if necessary change how you display the content. The process of evaluating one version against another version of the same web page is called *A/B testing*.

Listing Data

Websites have used lists for decades to convey related or hierarchical information. In Figure 5-3, you can see an older version of Yahoo.com that uses bulleted lists to display various categories and today's Allrecipes.com recipe page, which uses lists to display various ingredients.

Lists begin with a symbol, an indentation, and then the list item. The symbol used can be a number, letter, bullet, or no symbol at all.

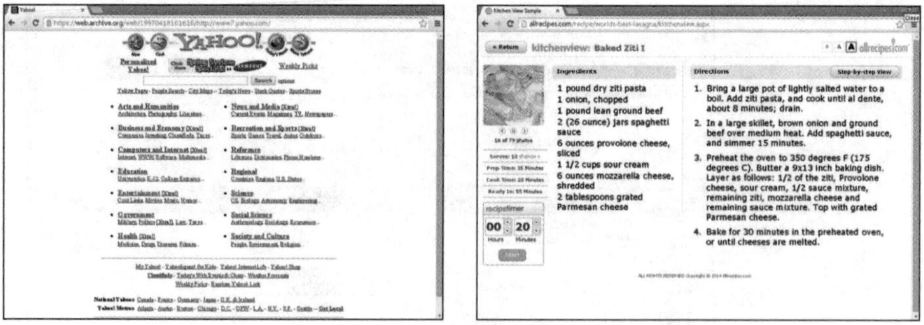

FIGURE 5-3:
Yahoo's 1997
homepage
using an
unordered
list (left) and
Allrecipes.
com's 2014
recipe using
an ordered list
(right).

Creating ordered and unordered lists

The two most popular types of lists are:

>> **Ordered:** Ordered lists are numerical or alphabetical lists in which the sequence of list items is important.

>> **Unordered:** These lists are usually bulleted lists in which the sequence of list items has no importance.

You create lists by specifying the type of list as ordered or unordered, and then adding each list item using the li tag, as shown in the following steps:

1. **Specify the type of list.**

Add opening and closing list tags that specify either an ordered (ol) or unordered (ul) list, as follows:

- ol to specify the beginning and end of an ordered list.

- ul to specify the beginning and end of an unordered list.

2. **Add an opening and closing tag (that is, ‹li› and ‹/li›) for each item in the list.**

For example, here's an ordered list:

```
<ol>
    <li> List item #1 </li>
    <li> List item #2 </li>
    <li> List item #3 </li>
</ol>
```

Nesting lists

Additionally, you can nest lists within lists. A list of any type can be nested inside another list; to nest a list, replace the list item tag ‹li› with a list type tag, either ‹ol› or ‹ul›.

The example code in Figure 5-4 shows various lists types including a nested list. (See Figures 5-4 and 5-5.)

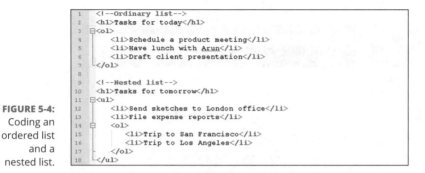

```
1   <!--Ordinary list-->
2   <h1>Tasks for today</h1>
3   <ol>
4       <li>Schedule a product meeting</li>
5       <li>Have lunch with Arun</li>
6       <li>Draft client presentation</li>
7   </ol>
8
9   <!--Nested list-->
10  <h1>Tasks for tomorrow</h1>
11  <ul>
12      <li>Send sketches to London office</li>
13      <li>File expense reports</li>
14      <ol>
15          <li>Trip to San Francisco</li>
16          <li>Trip to Los Angeles</li>
17      </ol>
18  </ul>
```

FIGURE 5-4: Coding an ordered list and a nested list.

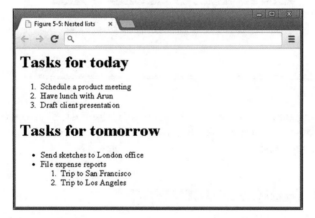

FIGURE 5-5: The page produced by the code in Figure 5-4.

The <h1> tag shown in this code sample is not necessary to create a list. I use it here only to name each list.

TIP

Every opening list or list item tag must be followed with a closing list or list item tag.

Putting Data in Tables

Tables help further organize text and tabular data on the page. (See Figure 5-6.) The table format is especially appropriate when displaying pricing information, comparing features across products, or in any situation where the columns or rows share a common attribute. Tables act as containers, and can hold and display any type of content, including text, such as heading and lists, and images. For example, the table in Figure 5-6 includes additional content and styling like icons at the top of each column, gray background shading, and rounded buttons. This content and styling can make tables you see online differ from tables you ordinarily see in books.

FIGURE 5-6:
Box.net uses tables to display pricing information.

TIP

Avoid using tables to create page layouts. In the past, developers created multi-column layouts using tables, but today developers use CSS (see Chapter 7) for layout-related tasks.

Basic table structuring

Tables are comprised of several parts, like the one shown in Figure 5-7.

FIGURE 5-7:
The different parts of a table.

You create a table by using the following basic steps:

1. **Define a table with the `table` element.**

To do this, add the opening and closing `<table>` tags.

2. **Divide the table into rows with the `tr` element.**

Between the opening and closing `table` tags, create opening `<tr>` tags and closing `</tr>` tags for each row of your table.

3. **Divide rows into cells using the `td` element.**

Between the opening and closing `tr` tags, create opening and closing `td` tags for each cell in the row.

4. **Highlight cells that are headers using the `th` element.**

Finally, specify any cells that are headers by replacing the `td` element with a `th` element.

REMEMBER

Your table will have only one opening and closing `<table>` tag; however, you can have one or more table rows (`tr`) and cells (`td`).

The following example code shows the syntax for creating the table shown in Figure 5-7.

```
<Table>
    <tr>
      <th>Table header 1</th>
      <th>Table header 2</th>
    </tr>
    <tr>
      <td>Row #1, Cell #1</td>
      <td>Row #1, Cell #2</td>
    </tr>
    <tr>
      <td>Row #2, Cell #1</td>
      <td>Row #2, Cell #2</td>
    </tr>
</table>
```

TIP

After you've decided how many rows and columns your table will have, make sure to use an opening and closing `<tr>` tag for each row, and an opening and closing `<td>` tag for each cell in the row.

Stretching table columns and rows

Take a look at the table describing Facebook's income statement in Figure 5-8. Data for 2011, 2012, and 2013 appears in individual columns of equal-sized width. Now look at Total Revenue, which appears in a cell that stretches or spans across several columns.

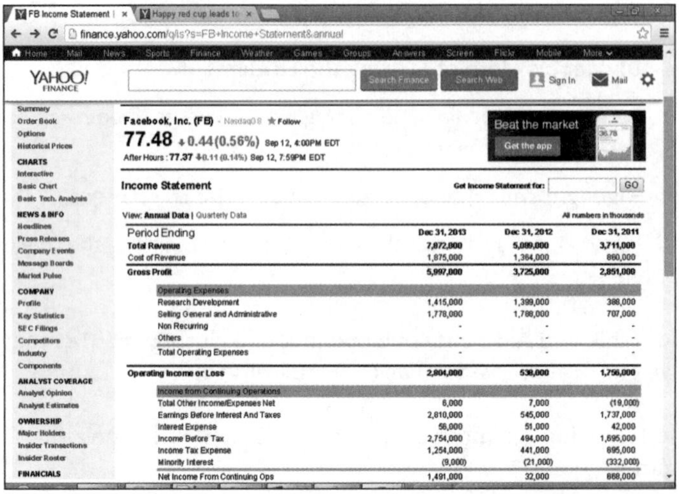

FIGURE 5-8:
An income statement in a table with columns of different sizes.

Stretching a cell across columns or rows is called *spanning*.

The `colspan` attribute spans a column over subsequent vertical columns. The value of the `colspan` attribute is set equal to the number of columns you want to span. You always span a column from left to right. Similarly, the `rowspan` attribute spans a row over subsequent horizontal rows. Set `rowspan` equal to the number of rows you want to span.

The following code generates a part of the table shown in Figure 5-8. You can see the `colspan` attribute spans the Total Revenue cell across two columns. As described in Chapter 4, the `<strong>` tag is used to mark important text, and is shown as bold by the browser.

```
<tr>
  <td colspan="2">
    <strong>Total Revenue</strong>
  </td>
  <td>
    <strong>7,872,000</strong>
  </td>
```

```
        <td>
            <strong>5,089,000</strong>
        </td>
        <td>
            <strong>3,711,000</strong>
        </td>
    </tr>
```

REMEMBER

If you set a column or row to span by more columns or rows than are actually present in the table, the browser will insert additional columns or rows, changing your table layout.

TIP

CSS helps size individual columns and rows, as well as entire tables. See Chapter 7.

Aligning tables and cells

WARNING

The latest version of HTML does not support the tags and attributes in this section. Although your browser may correctly render this code, there is no guarantee your browser will correctly render it in the future. I include these attributes because as of this writing, HTML code on the Internet, including the Yahoo Finance site in the previous examples, still use these deprecated (older) attributes in tables. This code is similar to expletives — recognize them but try not to use them. Refer to Chapter 6 to see modern techniques using Cascading Style Sheets (CSS) for achieving the identical effects.

The `table` element has three deprecated attributes to know — `align`, `width`, and `border`. These attributes are described in Table 5-1.

TABLE 5-1   **Table Attributes Replaced by CSS**

Attribute Name	Possible Values	Description
align	left center right	Position of table relative to the containing document according to the value of the attribute. For example, `align="right"` positions the table on the right side of the web page.
width	pixels (#) %	Width of table measured either in pixels on-screen or as a percentage of the browser window or container tag.
border	pixels (#)	Width of table border in pixels.

The following example code shows the syntax for creating the table in Figure 5-9 with align, width, and border attributes.

```
<Table align="right" width=50% border=1>
  <tr>
    <td>The Social Network</td>
    <td>Generation Like</td>
  </tr>
  <tr>
    <td>Tron</td>
    <td>War Games</td>
  </tr>
</table>
```

| The Social Network | Generation Like |
| Tron | War Games |

FIGURE 5-9: A table with deprecated align, width, and border attributes.

REMEMBER Always insert attributes inside the opening <html> tag, and enclose words in quotes.

The tr element has two deprecated attributes to know—align, and valign. These are described in Table 5-2.

The td element has four deprecated attributes to know—align, valign, width, and height. These are described in Table 5-3.

The following example code shows the syntax for creating the table in Figure 5-10 with align, valign, width, and height attributes.

```
<Table align="right" width=50% border=1>
  <tr align="right" valign="bottom">
    <td height=100>The Social Network</td>
```

```
        <td>Generation Like</td>
    </tr>
    <tr>
        <td height=200 align="center" valign="middle">Tron</td>
        <td align="center" valign="top" width=20%>War Games</td>
    </tr>
</table>
```

TABLE 5-2   **Table Row Attributes Replaced by CSS**

Attribute Name	Possible Values	Description
align	left right center justify	Horizontal alignment of a row's cell contents according to the value of the attribute. For example, align="right" positions a row's cell contents on the right side of each cell.
valign	top middle bottom	Vertical alignment of a row's cell contents according to the value of the attribute. For example, align="bottom" positions a row's cell contents on the bottom of each cell.

TABLE 5-3   **Table Cell Attributes Replaced by CSS**

Attribute Name	Possible Values	Description
align	left right center justify	Horizontal alignment of a cell's contents according to the value of the attribute. For example, align="center" positions the cell's contents in the center of the cell.
valign	top middle bottom	Vertical alignment of a cell's contents according to the value of the attribute. For example, align="middle" positions a cell's contents in the middle of the cell.
width	pixels (#) %	Width of a cell measured either in pixels on-screen or as a percentage of the table width.
height	pixels (#) %	Height of a cell measured either in pixels on-screen or as a percentage of the table width.

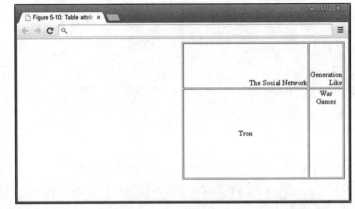

Figure 5-10: Table attrib ×

The Social Network | Generation Like

War Games

Tron

FIGURE 5-10:
A table with deprecated align, valign, width, and height attributes.

WARNING

Remember, these attributes are no longer supported and should not be used in your code.

Filling Out Forms

Forms allow you to capture input from your website visitors. Until now we have displayed content as-is, but capturing input from visitors allows you to:

>> **Modify existing content on the page.** For example, price and date filters on airline websites allow for finding a desired flight more quickly.

>> **Store the input for later use.** For example, a website may use a registration form to collect your email, username, and password information to allow you to access it at a later date.

Understanding how forms work

Forms pass information entered by a user to a server by using the following process:

1. The browser displays a form on the client machine.

2. The user completes the form and presses the submit button.

3. The browser submits the data collected from the form to a server.

4. The server processes and stores the data and sends a response to the client machine.

5. The browser displays the response, usually indicating whether the submission was successful.

See Chapter 2 for an additional discussion about the relationship between the client and server.

A full description of how the server receives and stores data (Steps 3 to 5) is beyond the scope of this book. For now, all you need to know is that server-side programming languages such as Python, PHP, and Ruby are used to write scripts that receive and store form submissions.

Forms are very flexible, and can record a variety of user inputs. Input fields used in forms can include free text fields, radio buttons, checkboxes, drop-down menus, range sliders, dates, phone numbers, and more. (See Table 5-4.) Additionally, input fields can be set to initial default values without any user input.

TABLE 5-4   **Selected Form Attributes**

Attribute Name	Possible Values	Description
type	checkbox email submit text password radio (a complete list of values has been omitted here for brevity)	Defines the type of input field to display in the form. For example, text is used for free text fields, and submit is used to create a submit button.
value	*text*	The initial value of the input control.

View the entire list of form input types and example code at www.w3schools.com/tags/att_input_type.asp.

Creating basic forms

You create a basic form by

1. Defining a form with the form element.

Start by adding an opening ‹form› tag and closing ‹/form› tag.

2. Using the `action` attribute, specify in the `form` element where to send form data.

Add an `action` attribute to your opening `<form>` tag and set it equal to the URL of a script that will process and store the user input.

3. Using the `method` attribute, specify in the `form` element how to send form data.

Add a `method` attribute to your opening `<form>` tag and set it equal to POST.

TECHNICAL
STUFF

The `method` attribute is set equal to GET or POST. The technicalities of each are beyond the scope of this book, but, in general, POST is used for storing sensitive information (such as credit card numbers), whereas GET is used to allow users to bookmark or share with others the results of a submitted form (such as, for example, airline flight listings).

4. Providing a way for users to input and submit responses with the `input` element.

Between the opening `<form>` and closing `</form>` tags, create one `<input>` tag.

REMEMBER

Your form will have only one opening and closing `<form>` tag; however, you will have at least two `<input>` tags to collect and submit user data.

5. Specify input types using the `type` attribute in the `input` element.

For this example, set the `type` attribute equal to "text".

TIP

The `<input>` tag does not have a closing tag, which is an exception to the "close every tag you open" rule. These tags are called self-closing tags, and you can see more examples in Chapter 4.

6. Finally, create another `<input>` tag and set the `type` attribute equal to `submit`.

The following example code shows the syntax for creating the form shown in Figure 5-11.

```
<form action="mailto:nikhil.abraham@gmail.com" method="POST">
    <input type="text" value="Type a short message here">
    <input type="submit">
</form>
```

TECHNICAL
STUFF

The `action` attribute in this form is set equal to `mailto`, which signals to the browser to send an email using your default mail client (such as Outlook or Gmail). If your browser is not configured to handle email links, then this form won't work. Ordinarily, forms are submitted to a server to process and store the form's contents, but in this example form the contents are submitted to the user's email application.

FIGURE 5-11:
A form with one user input and a submit button.

Practicing More with HTML

Practice your HTML online using the Codecademy website. Codecademy is a free website created in 2011 to allow anyone to learn how to code right in the browser, without installing or downloading any software. Practice all of the tags (and a few more) that you learned in this chapter by following these steps:

1. **Open your browser, go to** www.dummies.com/go/coding, **and click on the link to Codecademy.**

2. **Sign in to your Codecademy account.**

   Signing up is discussed in Chapter 3. Creating an account allows you to save your progress as you work, but it's optional.

3. **Navigate to and click on HTML Basics II to practice creating lists, and HTML Basics III to practice creating tables.**

4. **Background information is presented in the upper left portion of the site, and instructions are presented in the lower left portion of the site.**

5. **Complete the instructions in the main coding window. As you type, a live preview of your code is generated.**

6. **After you have finished completing the instructions, click the Save and Submit Code button.**

   If you have followed the instructions correctly, a green checkmark appears, and you proceed to the next exercise. If an error exists in your code a warning appears with a suggested fix. If you run into a problem or a bug you cannot fix, click on the hint, use the Q&A Forum, or tweet me at @nikhilgabraham and include hashtag #codingFD.

Chapter 6

Getting Stylish with CSS

Create your own style . . . let it be unique for yourself and yet identifiable for others.

— ANNA WINTOUR

The website code examples I have shown you in the preceding chapters resemble websites you may have seen from a previous era. Websites you browse today are different, and have a more polished look and feel. Numerous factors enabled this change. Twenty years ago you might have browsed the Internet with a dial-up modem, but today you likely use a very fast Internet connection and a more powerful computer. Programmers have used this extra bandwidth and speed to write code to further customize and style websites.

In this chapter you learn modern techniques to style websites using Cascading Style Sheets (CSS). First, I discuss basic CSS structure, and then the CSS rules to style your content. Finally, I show you how to apply these rules to your websites.

What Does CSS Do?

CSS styles HTML elements with greater control than just using HTML. Take a look at Figure 6-1. On the left, Facebook appears as it currently exists; on the right, however, the same Facebook page is shown without all the CSS styling. Without the CSS, all the images and text appear left-justified, borders and shading disappear, and text has minimal formatting.

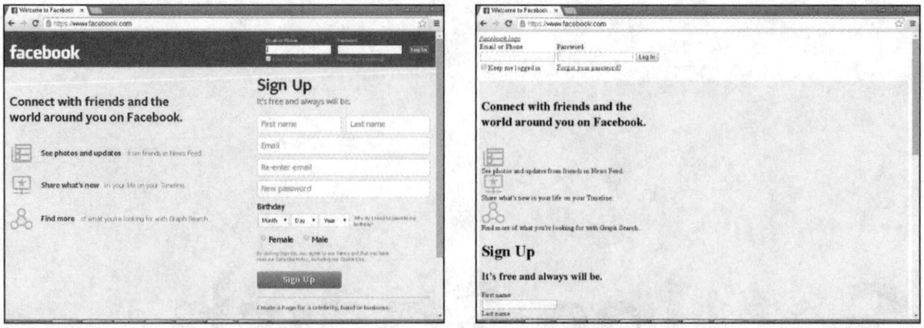

FIGURE 6-1:
Left Facebook with CSS. Right: Facebook without CSS.

CSS can style almost any HTML tag that creates a visible element on the page, including all the HTML tags used to create headings, paragraphs, links, images, lists, and tables that I showed you in previous chapters. Specifically, CSS allows you to style:

» Text size, color, style, typeface, and alignment

» Link color and style

» Image size and alignment

» List bullet styles and indentation

» Table size, shading, borders, and alignment

REMEMBER

CSS styles and positions the HTML elements that appear on a web page. However, some HTML elements (such as, for example, ⟨head⟩) are not visible on the page and are not styled using CSS.

You may wonder why creating a separate language like CSS to handle styling was considered a better approach than expanding the capabilities of HTML. There are three reasons:

» **History:** CSS was created four years after HTML as an experiment to see whether developers and consumers wanted extra styling effects. At the time, it was unclear whether CSS would be useful, and only some major browsers supported it. As a result, CSS was created separately from HTML to allow developers to build sites using just HTML.

>> **Code management:** Initially, some CSS functionality overlapped with existing HTML functionality. However, specifying styling effects in HTML results in cluttered and messy code. For example, specifying a particular font typeface in HTML requires that you include the font typeface attribute in every paragraph (`<p>`) tag. Styling a single paragraph this way is easy, but applying the font to a series of paragraphs (or an entire page or website) quickly becomes tedious. By contrast, CSS requires the typeface to be specified only once, and it automatically applies to all paragraphs. This feature makes it easier for developers to write and maintain code. In addition, separating the styling of the content from the actual content itself has allowed search engines and other automated website agents to more easily process the content on web pages.

>> **Inertia:** Currently millions of web pages use HTML and CSS separately, and every day that number grows. CSS started as a separate language for reasons stated above, and it remains a separate language because its popularity continues to grow.

CSS Structure

CSS follows a set of rules to ensure that websites will be displayed in the same way no matter the browser or computer used. Sometimes, because of varying support of the CSS standard, browsers can and do display web pages differently. Nevertheless, generally speaking, CSS ensures that users have a consistent experience across all browsers.

TIP

You can use any browser to see CSS you write style your HTML files, though I strongly recommend you download, install, and use Chrome or Firefox.

Choosing the element to style

CSS continues to evolve and support increased functionality, but the basic syntax for defining CSS rules remains the same. CSS modifies HTML elements with rules that apply to each element. These rules are written as follows:

```
selector {
  property: value;
}
```

A CSS rule is comprised of three parts:

>> **Selector:** The HTML element you want to style.

>> **Property:** The feature of the HTML element you want to style, such as, for example, font typeface, image height, or color.

>> **Value:** The options for the property that the CSS rule sets. For example, if color was the property, the value could be red.

The selector identifies which HTML element you want to style. In HTML, an element is surrounded by angle brackets, but in CSS the selector stands alone. The selector is followed by a space, an opening left curly bracket ({), property with a value, and then a closing right curly bracket (}). The line break after the opening curly bracket, and before the closing curly bracket is not required by CSS — in fact, you could put all your code on one line with no line breaks or spaces. Using line breaks is convention followed by developers to make CSS easier to modify and read.

TIP

You can find curly brackets on most keyboards to the right of the P key.

The following code shows you an example of CSS modifying a specific HTML element. The CSS code appears first, followed by the HTML code that it modifies:

The CSS:

```
h1 {
    font-family: cursive;
}
```

And now the HTML:

```
<h1>
    Largest IPOs in US History
</h1>
<ul>
    <li>2014: Alibaba - $20B</li>
    <li>2008: Visa - $18B</li>
</ul>
```

The CSS selector targets and styles the HTML element with the same name (in this case, <h1> tags). For example, in Figure 6-2, the heading "Largest IPOs in US History," created using the opening and closing <h1> tag is styled using the h1 selector, and the font-family property with cursive value.

FIGURE 6-2:
CSS targeting
the heading h1
element.

REMEMBER

CSS uses a colon instead of the equals sign (=) to set values against properties.

TIP

The font in Figure 6-2 likely does not appear to be cursive, as defined in the code above, because cursive is the name of a generic font family, and not a specific font. Generic font families are described later in this chapter.

My property has value

CSS syntax requires that a CSS property and its value appear within opening and closing curly brackets. After each property is a colon, and after each value is a semi-colon. This combination of property and value together is called a *declaration*, and a group of properties and values is called a *declaration block*.

Let us look at a specific example with multiple properties and values:

```
h1 {
    font-size: 15px;
    color: blue;
}
```

In this example, CSS styles the h1 element, changing the font-size property to 15px, and the color property to blue.

TIP

You can improve the readability of your code by putting each declaration (each property/value combination) on its own line. Additionally, adding spaces or tabs to indent the declarations also improves the readability. Adding these line breaks and indentions doesn't affect browser performance in any way, but it will make it easier for you and others to read your code.

Hacking the CSS on your favorite website

In Chapter 2, you modified a news website's HTML code. In this chapter, you modify its CSS. Let's take a look at some CSS rules in the wild. In this example, you change the CSS on huffingtonpost.com (or your news website of choice) using the Chrome browser. Just follow these steps:

1. **Using a Chrome browser, navigate to your favorite news website, ideally one with many headlines. (See Figure 6-3.)**

2. **Place your mouse pointer over a headline, right-click, and from the menu that appears select Inspect Element.**

A window opens at the bottom of your browser.

3. **Click the Style tab on the right side of this window to see the CSS rules being applied to HTML elements. (See Figure 6-4.)**

4. **Change the color of the headline using CSS. To do this, first find the** color **property in the** element.style **section; note the square color box within that property that displays a sample of the current color. Click on this box and change the value by selecting a new color from the pop-up menu, and then press Enter.**

Your headline now appears in the color you picked. (See Figure 6-5.)

If the element.style section is blank and no color property appears, you can still add it manually. To do so, click once in the element.style section, and when the blinking cursor appears, type color: purple. The headline changes to purple.

TIP

FIGURE 6-4:
The CSS rules that style the Huffington Post website.

FIGURE 6-5:
Changing the CSS changes the color of the headline.

TIP

As with HTML, you can modify any website's CSS using Chrome's Inspect Element feature, also known as Developer Tools. Most modern browsers, including Firefox, Safari, and Opera, have a similar feature.

Common CSS Tasks and Selectors

Although CSS includes over 150 properties, and many values for each property, on modern websites a handful of CSS properties and values do the majority of the work. In the previous section, when you "hacked" the CSS on a live website, you changed the heading color — a common task in CSS. Other common tasks performed with CSS include:

>> Changing font size, style, font family, and decoration

>> Customizing links including color, background color, and link state

>> Adding background images and formatting foreground images

Font gymnastics: size, color, style, family, and decoration

CSS lets you control text in many HTML elements. The most common text-related CSS properties and values are shown in Table 6-1. I describe these properties and values more fully in the sections that follow.

TABLE 6-1   **Common CSS Properties and Values for Styling Text**

Property Name	Possible Values	Description
font-size	pixels (#px) % em (#em)	Specifies the size of text measured either in pixels, as a percentage of the containing element's font size, or with an em value which is calculated by desired pixel value divided by containing element font size in pixels. Example: font-size: 16px;
color	name hex code rgb value	Changes the color of the text specified using names (color: blue;), hexadecimal code (color: #0000FF;), or RGB (red, green, and blue) value (color: rgb(0,0,255);).
font-style	normal italic	Sets font to appear in italics (or not).
font-weight	normal bold	Sets font to appear as bold (or not).
font-family	font name	Sets the font typeface. Example: font-family: "serif";
text-decoration	none underline line-through	Sets font to have an underline or strikethrough (or not).

Setting the font-size

As in a word processor, you can set the size of the font you're using with CSS's `font-size` property. You have a few options for setting the font size, and the most common is to use pixels, as in the following:

```
p {
    font-size: 16px;
}
```

In this example, I used the p selector to size the paragraph text to 16 pixels. One disadvantage of using pixels to size your font occurs when users who prefer a large font size for readability have changed their browser settings to a default font size value that's larger than the one you specify on your site. In these situations, the font size specified in the browser takes precedence, and the fonts on your site will not scale to adjust to these preferences.

Percentage-sizing and em values, the other options to size your fonts, are considered more accessibility-friendly. The default browser font-size of normal text is 16 pixels. With percentage-sizing and em values, fonts can be sized relative to the user-specified default. For example, the CSS for percentage-sizing looks like this:

```
p {
    font-size: 150%;
}
```

In this example, I used the p selector to size the paragraph text to 150% of the default size. If the browser's default font size was set at 16 pixels, this paragraph's font would appear sized at 24 pixels (150% of 16).

TECHNICAL
STUFF

A `font-size` equal to 1px is equivalent to one pixel on your monitor, so the actual size of the text displayed varies according to the size of the monitor. Accordingly, for a fixed font size in pixels, the text appears smaller as you increase the screen resolution.

Setting the color

The `color` property sets the color in one of three ways:

» **Name:** 147 colors can be referenced by name. You can reference common colors, such as black, blue, and red, along with uncommon colors, such as burlywood, lemon chiffon, thistle, and rebeccapurple.

Rebecca Meyer, the daughter of prominent CSS standards author Eric Meyer, passed away in 2014 from brain cancer at the age of six. In response, the CSS standardization committee approved adding a shade of purple called rebecca-purple to the CSS specification in Rebecca's honor. All major Internet browsers have implemented support for the color.

>> **Hex code:** Colors can be defined by component parts of red, green, and blue, and when using hexadecimal code over 16 million colors can be referenced. In the code example, I set the h1 color equal to #FF0000. After the hashtag, the first two digits (FF) refers to the red in the color, the next two digits (00) refers to the green in the color, and the final two digits (00) refers to the blue in the color.

>> **RGB value:** Just like hex codes, RGB values specify the red, green, and blue component parts for over 16 million colors. RGB values are the decimal equivalent to hexadecimal values.

Don't worry about trying to remember hex codes or RGB values. You can easily identify colors using an online color picker such as the one at www.w3schools.com/tags/ref_colorpicker.asp.

The following example shows all three types of color changes:

```
p {
  color: red
}
h1 {
  color: #FF0000
}
li {
  color: rgb(255,0,0)
}
```

li is the element name for a list item in ordered or unordered lists.

All three colors in the code example above reference the same shade of red. For the full list of colors that can be referenced by name see here: www.w3.org/TR/css3-color/#svg-color.

Setting the font-style and font-weight

The font-style property can set text to italics, and the font-weight property can set text to bold. For each of these properties, the default is normal, which doesn't need to be specified. In the example below, the paragraph is styled so the font appears italicized and bold. Here's an example of each:

```
p {
  font-style: italics;
  font-weight: bold;
}
```

Setting the font-family

The `font-family` property sets the typeface used for text. The property is set equal to one font, or to a list of fonts separated by commas. Your website visitors will have a variety of different fonts installed on their computers, but the `font-family` property displays your specified font only if that font is already installed on their system.

The `font-family` property can be set equal to two types of values:

>> **Font name:** Specific font names such as Times New Roman, Arial, and Courier.

>> **Generic font family:** Modern browsers usually define one installed font for each generic font family. These five generic font families include

  • `serif` (Times New Roman, Palantino)

  • `sans-serif` (Helvetica, Verdana)

  • `monospace` (Courier, Andale Mono)

  • `cursive` (Comic Sans, Florence)

  • `fantasy` (Impact, Oldtown)

When using `font-family` it's best to define two or three specific fonts followed by a generic font family as a fallback in case the fonts you specify aren't installed, as in the following example:

```
p {
  font-family: "Times New Roman", Helvetica, serif;
}
```

In this example, the paragraph's font family is defined as Times New Roman. If Times New Roman isn't installed on the user's computer, the browser then uses Helvetica. If Helvetica is not installed, the browser will use any available font in the generic serif font family.

When using a font name with multiple words (such as Times New Roman) enclose the font name in quotes.

Setting the text-decoration

The `text-decoration` property sets any font underlining or strikethrough. By default, the property is equal to none, which does not have to be specified. In the following example, any text with an h1 heading is underlined whereas any text inside a paragraph tag is made strikethrough:

```
h1 {
    text-decoration: underline;
}
p {
    text-decoration: line-through;
}
```

Customizing links

In general, browsers display links as blue underlined text. Originally, this default behavior minimized the confusion between content on the page and an interactive link. Today, almost every website styles links in its own way. Some websites don't underline links; others retain the underlining but style links in colors other than blue, and so on.

The HTML anchor element (a) is used to create links. The text between the opening and closing anchor tag is the link description, and the URL set in the `href` attribute is the address the browser visits when the link is clicked.

The anchor tag has evolved over time and today has four states:

>> **link:** A link that a user has not clicked or visited.

>> **visited:** A link that a user has clicked or visited.

>> **hover:** A link that the user hovers the mouse cursor over without clicking.

>> **active:** A link the user has begun to click but hasn't yet released the mouse button.

CSS can style each of these four states, most often by using the properties and values shown in Table 6-2.

TABLE 6-2

Common CSS Properties and Values for Styling Links

Property Name	Possible Values	Description
color	name hex code rgb value	Link color specified using names (color: blue;), hexadecimal code (color: #0000FF;), or RGB value (color: rgb(0,0,255);).
text-decoration	none underline	Sets link to have an underline (or not).

The following example styles links in a way that's similar to the way they're styled in articles at Wikipedia, where links appear blue by default, underlined on mouse hover, and orange when active. As shown in Figure 6-6, the first link to Chief Technology Officer of the United States appears underlined as it would if my mouse was hovering over it. Also, the link to Google appears orange as it would if active and my mouse was clicking it.

```
a:link{
    color: rgb(6,69,173);
    text-decoration: none;
}
a:visited {
    color: rgb(11,0,128)
}
a:hover {
    text-decoration: underline
}
a:active {
    color: rgb(250,167,0)
}
```

REMEMBER

Remember to include the colon between the a selector and the link state.

TECHNICAL STUFF

Although explaining why is out of the scope of this book, CSS specifications insist that you define the various link states in the order shown here — link, visited, hover, and then active. However, it is acceptable to not define a link state, as long as this order is preserved.

The various link states are known as *pseudo-class selectors*. Pseudo-class selectors add a keyword to CSS selectors and allow you to style a special state of the selected element.

FIGURE 6-6:
Wikipedia.org page showing link, visited, hover, and active states.

Adding background images and styling foreground images

You can use CSS to add background images behind HTML elements. Most commonly, the `background-image` property is used to add background images to individual HTML elements such as `div`, `table`, and `p`, or (when applied to the `body` element) to entire web pages.

TIP

Background images with smaller file sizes load more quickly than larger images. This is especially important if your visitors commonly browse your website using a mobile phone, which typically has a slower data connection.

The properties and values in Table 6-3 show the options for adding background images.

Setting the background-image

As shown in the following example, the `background-image` property can set the background image for the entire web page or a specific element.

```
body {
    background-image:
    url("http://upload.wikimedia.org/wikipedia/commons/e/e5/Chrysler_Building_Midtown_
        Manhattan_New_York_City_1932.jpg ");
}
```

TABLE 6-3   **CSS Properties and Values for Background Images**

Property Name	Possible Values	Description
background-image	url("*URL*")	Adds a background image from the image link specified at *URL*.
background-size	auto contain cover *width height* (#px, %)	Sets background size according to the value: auto (default value) displays the image as originally sized. contain scales the image's width and height so that it fits inside element. cover scales the image so element background is not visible. Background size can also be set by specifying width and height in pixels or as a percentage.
background-position	*keywords* *position (#px, %)*	Positions the background in element using keywords or exact position. *Keywords* are comprised of horizontal keywords (left, right, center), and vertical keywords (top, center, and bottom). The placement of the background can also be exactly defined using pixels or a percentage to describe the horizontal and vertical position relative to the element.
background-repeat	repeat repeat-x repeat-y no-repeat	Sets the background image to *tile*, or repeat, as follows: horizontally (repeat-x) vertically (repeat-y) horizontally and vertically (repeat) don't repeat at all (no-repeat).
background-attachment	scroll fixed	Sets the background to scroll with other content (scroll), or to remain fixed (fixed).

TIP

You can find background images at sites such as images.google.com, www.flickr.com, or publicdomainarchive.com.

WARNING

Check image copyright information to see if you have permission to use the image, and comply with image's licensing terms, which can include attributing or identifying the author. Additionally, directly linking to images on other servers is called *hotlinking*. It is preferable to download the image, and host and link to the image on your own server.

TIP

If you'd prefer a single-color background instead of an image, use the `background-color` property. This property is defined in much the same way as the `background-image` property. Just set it equal to a color name, RGB value, or hex code, as I describe earlier in this chapter in the section "Setting the color."

Setting the background-size

By specifying exact dimensions using pixels or percentages, the `background-size` property can scale background images to be smaller or larger, as needed. In addition, this property has three dimensions commonly used on web pages, as follows (see Figure 6-7):

» **auto:** This value maintains the original dimensions of an image.

» **cover:** This value scales an image so all dimensions are greater than or equal to the size of the container or HTML element.

» **contain:** This value scales an image so all dimensions are less than or equal to the size of the container or HTML element.

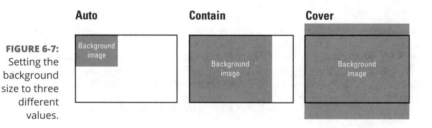

FIGURE 6-7: Setting the background size to three different values.

Setting the background-position

The `background-position` sets the initial position of the background image. The default initial position is in the top left corner of the web page or specific element. You change the default position by specifying a pair of keyword or position values, as follows:

» **Keywords:** The first keyword (`left`, `center`, or `right`) represents the horizontal position, and the second keyword (`top`, `center`, or `bottom`) represents the vertical position.

» **Position:** The first position value represents the horizontal position, and the second value represents the vertical. Each value is defined using pixels or percentages, representing the distance from the top-left of the browser or the specified element. For example, `background-position: center center` is equal to `background-position: 50% 50%`. (See Figure 6-8.)

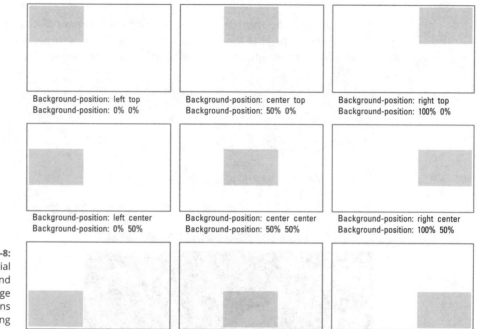

Setting the background-repeat

The `background-repeat` property sets the direction the background will tile as follows:

>> **repeat:** This value (the default) repeats the background image both horizontally and vertically.

>> **repeat-x:** This value repeats the background image only horizontally.

>> **repeat-y:** This repeats the background image only vertically.

>> **no-repeat:** This value prevents the background from repeating at all.

Setting the background-attachment

The `background-attachment` property sets the background image to move (or not) when the user scrolls through content on the page. The property can be set to:

>> **scroll:** The background image moves when the user scrolls.

>> **fixed:** The background image does not move when the user scrolls.

The following code segment uses several of the properties discussed earlier to add a background image that stretches across the entire web page, is aligned in the center, does not repeat, and does not move when the user scrolls. (See Figure 6-9.)

```
body {
    background-image: url("http://upload.wikimedia.org/wikipedia/commons/thumb/a/a0/
        USMC-090807-M-8097K-022.jpg/640px-USMC-090807-M-8097K-022.jpg");
    background-size: cover;
    background-position: center center;
    background-repeat: no-repeat;
    background-attachment: fixed;
}
```

FIGURE 6-9:
An image set as the background for entire page.

Styling Me Pretty

The CSS rules discussed in this chapter give you a taste of a few common styling properties and values. Although you aren't likely to remember every property and value, with practice the property and value names will come to you naturally. After you understand the basic syntax, the next step is to actually incorporate CSS into your web page and try your hand at styling HTML elements.

Adding CSS to your HTML

There are three ways to apply CSS to a website to style HTML elements:

» **In-line CSS:** CSS can be specified within an HTML file on the same line as the HTML element it styles. This method requires placing the `style` attribute inside the opening HTML tag. Generally, in-line CSS is the least preferred way of styling a website because the styling rules are frequently repeated. Here's an example of in-line CSS:

```
<!DOCTYPE html>
<html>
<head>
    <title>Record IPOs</title>
</head>
<body>
    <h1 style="color: red;">Alibaba IPO expected to be biggest IPO of all time</h1>
</body>
</html>
```

» **Embedded CSS:** With this approach, CSS appears within the HTML file, but separated from the HTML tags it modifies. The CSS code appears within the HTML file between an opening and closing `<style>` tag, which itself is located between an opening and closing `<head>` tag. Embedded CSS is usually used when styling a single HTML page differently than the rest of your website.

In this example, the embedded CSS styles the header red, just like the in-line CSS does above.

```
<!DOCTYPE html>
<html>
<head>
    <title>Record IPOs</title>
    <style type="text/css">
    h1 {
        color: red;
    }
    </style>
</head>
<body>
    <h1>Alibaba IPO expected to be biggest IPO of all time</h1>
</body>
</html>
```

» **Separate style sheets:** CSS can be specified in a separate *style sheet* — that is, in a separate file. Using a separate style sheet is the preferred approach to storing your CSS because it makes maintaining the HTML file easier and allows you to quickly make changes. In the HTML file, the `<link>` tag is used to refer to the separate style sheet, and has three attributes:

- `href`: Specifies the CSS filename.
- `rel`: Should be set equal to `"stylesheet"`.
- `type`: Should be set equal to `"text/css"`.

TECHNICAL STUFF

With three different ways of styling HTML elements with CSS, all three ways could be used with contradictory styles. For example, say your in-line CSS styles h1 elements as red, whereas embedded CSS styles them as blue, and a separate style sheet styles them as green. To resolve these conflicts, in-line CSS has the highest priority and overrides any other CSS rules. If no in-line CSS is specified, then embedded CSS has the next highest priority, and finally in the absence of in-line or embedded CSS, the styles in a separate style sheet are used. In the example, with the presence of all three styles, the h1 element text would appear red because in-line CSS has the highest priority and overrides the embedded CSS blue styling, and the separate CSS green styling.

The following example uses a separate CSS style sheet to style the header red, as in the previous two examples:

CSS: style.css

```
h1 {
    color: red;
}
```

HTML: index.html

```
<DOCTYPE html>
<html>
<head>
 <title>Record IPOs</title>
 <link href="style.css" text="text/css" rel="stylesheet">
</head>
<body>
  <h1>Alibaba IPO expected to be biggest IPO of all time</h1>
</body>
</html>
```

Building your first web page

Practice your HTML online using the Codecademy website. Codecademy is a free website created in 2011 to allow anyone to learn how to code right in the browser, without installing or downloading any software. You can practice all of the tags (and a few more) discussed in this chapter by following these steps:

1. **Open your browser, go to** www.dummies.com/go/codingfd, **and click on the Codecademy link.**

2. **Sign in to your Codecademy account.**

   Signing up is discussed in Chapter 3. Creating an account allows you to save your progress as you work, but it's optional.

3. **Navigate to and click on Get Started with HTML.**

4. **Background information is presented in the upper left portion of the site, and instructions are presented in the lower left portion of the site.**

5. **Complete the instructions in the main coding window. As you type, a live preview of your code is generated.**

6. **After you have finished completing the instructions, click the Save and Submit Code button.**

   If you have followed the instructions correctly, a green checkmark appears, and you proceed to the next exercise. If an error exists in your code a warning appears with a suggested fix. If you run into a problem, or have a bug you cannot fix, click on the hint, use the Q&A Forums, or tweet me at @nikhilgabraham and include hashtag #codingFD.

Chapter 7

Next Steps with CSS

Design is not just what it looks like and feels like. Design is how it works.
—STEVE JOBS

In this chapter, you continue building on the CSS you learned in the previous chapter. So far, the CSS rules you've seen applied to the entire web page, but now they get more specific. You learn how to style several more HTML elements, including lists, tables, and forms, and how to select and style specific parts of a web page, such as the first paragraph in a story or the last row of a table. Finally, you learn how professional web developers use CSS and the box model to control down to the pixel the positioning of elements on the page. Understanding the box model is not necessary to build our app in Chapter 10.

Before diving in, remember the big picture: HTML puts content on the web page, and CSS further styles and positions that content. Instead of trying to memorize every rule, use this chapter to understand CSS basics. CSS selectors have properties and values that modify HTML elements. There is no better way to learn than by doing, so feel free to skip ahead to the Codecademy practice lessons at the end of the chapter. Then, use this chapter as a reference when you have questions about specific elements you are trying to style.

Styling (More) Elements on Your Page

In this section, you discover common ways to style lists and tables. In the previous chapter, the CSS properties and rules you learned like `color` and `font-family` can apply to any HTML element containing text. By contrast, some of the CSS shown here is used only to style lists, tables, and forms.

Styling lists

In Chapter 5 you learned how to create ordered lists, which start with markers like letters or numbers, and unordered lists, which start with markers like bullet points. By default, list items in an ordered list use numbers (for example, 1, 2, 3), whereas list items in unordered lists use a solid-black-circle (●).

These defaults may not be appropriate for all circumstances. In fact, the two most common tasks when styling a list include:

>> **Changing the marker used to create a list:** For unordered lists, like this one, you can use a solid disc, empty circle, or square bullet point. For ordered lists, you can use numbers, roman numerals (upper or lower case), or case letters (upper or lower).

>> **Specifying an image to use as the bullet point:** You can create your own marker for ordered and unordered lists instead of using the default option. For example, if you created an unordered bulleted list for a burger restaurant, instead of using a solid circle as a bullet point you could use a color hamburger icon image.

You can accomplish either of these tasks by using the properties in Table 7-1 with an `ol` or `ul` selector to modify the list type.

REMEMBER

CSS selectors using properties and rules modify HTML elements by the same name. For example, Figure 7-1 has HTML `<ul>` tags that are referred to in CSS with the `ul` selector, and styled using the properties and rules in Table 7-1.

TABLE 7-1 **Common CSS Properties and Values for Styling Lists**

Property Name	Possible Values	Description
`list-style-type` (unordered list)	disc circle square none	Sets the markers used to create list items in an unordered list to disc (●), circle (o), square (■), or none.

Property Name	Possible Values	Description
list-style-type (ordered list)	decimal upper-roman lower-roman upper-alpha lower-alpha	Sets the markers used to create list items in an ordered list to decimal (1, 2, 3), uppercase roman numerals (I, II, III), lowercase roman numerals (i, ii, iii), uppercase letters (A, B, C), or lowercase letters (a, b, c).
list-style-image	url("*URL*")	When *URL* is replaced with the image link sets an image as the marker used to create a list item.

TIP

Many text website navigation bars are created using unordered bulleted lists with the marker set to none. You can see an example in the Codecademy CSS Positioning course starting with exercise 21.

CSS properties and values apply to a CSS selector and modify an HTML element. In the following example, embedded CSS (between the opening and closing <style> tags) and in-line CSS (defined with the style attribute in the HTML) is used to:

» Change the marker in an unordered list to a square using list-style-type

» Change the marker in an ordered list to uppercase roman numerals again using list-style-type

» Set a custom marker to an icon using list-style-image

The code for this is shown below and in Figure 7-1. Figure 7-2 shows this code rendered in the browser.

```
<html>
<head>
<title>Figure 7-1: Lists</title>
<style>
ul {
    list-style-type: square;
}

ol {
    list-style-type: upper-roman;
}
```

```
li {
  font-size: 27px;
}

</style>
</head>
<body>

<h1>Ridesharing startups</h1>
<ul>
  <li>Hailo: book a taxi on your phone</li>
  <li>Lyft: request a peer to peer ride</li>
  <li style="list-style-image: url('car.png');">Uber: hire a driver</li>
</ul>

<h1>Food startups</h1>
<ol>
  <li>Grubhub: order takeout food online</li>
  <li style="list-style-image: url('burger.png');">Blue Apron: subscribe to weekly meal
  delivery</li>
  <li>Instacart: request groceries delivered the same day</li>
</ol>
</body>
</html>
```

```
<html>
<head>
<title>Figure 7-1: Lists</title>
<style>
ul {
   list-style-type: square;
}
ol {
   list-style-type: upper-roman;
}

li {
   font-size: 27px;
}
</style>
</head>
<body>
<h1>Ridesharing startups</h1>
<ul>
   <li>Hailo: book a taxi on your phone</li>
   <li>Lyft: request a peer to peer ride</li>
   <li style="list-style-image: url('car.png');">Uber: request a drivers for hire</li>
</ul>
<h1>Food startups</h1>
<ol>
   <li>Grubhub: order takeout food online</li>
   <li style="list-style-image: url('burger.png');">Blue Apron: subscribe to weekly meal
   delivery</li>
   <li>Instacart: request groceries delivered the same day</li>
</ol>
</body>
</html>
```

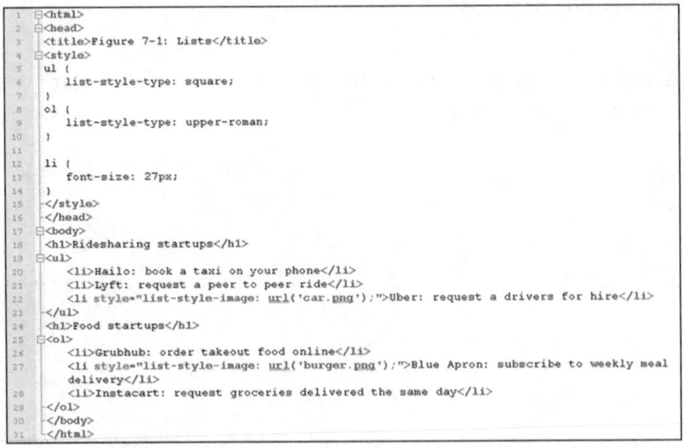

FIGURE 7-1: Embedded and in-line CSS.

TIP

If the custom image for your marker is larger than the text, your text may not align vertically with the marker. To fix this, you can either increase the font size of each list item using `font-size`, as shown in the example, increase the margin between each list item using `margin`, or set `list-style-type` to none and set a background image on the `ul` element using `background-image`.

REMEMBER

There are three ways to apply CSS — inline CSS using the `style` attribute, embedded CSS using an opening and closing `<style>` tag, and in a separate CSS style sheet.

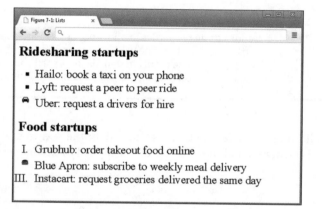

FIGURE 7-2:
Ordered and unordered lists modified to change the marker type.

Designing tables

In Chapter 5, you found out how to create basic tables. By default, the width of these tables expands to fit content inside the table, content in individual cells is left aligned, and no borders are displayed.

These defaults may not be appropriate for all circumstances. Deprecated (unsupported) HTML attributes can modify these defaults, but at any time browsers could stop recognizing these attributes, and any tables created with these attributes would display incorrectly. As a safer alternative, CSS can style tables with greater control. Three common tasks CSS can perform for tables include the following:

>> Setting the width of a table, table row, or individual table cell with the `width` property.

>> Aligning text within the table with the `text-align` property.

>> Displaying borders within the table with the `border` property. (See Table 7-2.)

TABLE 7-2 **Common CSS Properties and Values for Styling Tables**

Property Name	Possible Values	Description
width	*pixels* (#px) %	Width of table measured either in pixels on-screen or as a percentage of the browser window or container tag.
text-align	left right center justify	Position of text relative to the table according to the value of the attribute. For example, text-align="center" positions the text in the center of the table cell.
border	width style color	Defines three properties in one—border-width, border-style, and border-color. The values must be specified in this order: Width (pixel), style (none, dotted, dashed, solid), and color (name, hexadecimal code, RBG value). For example, border: 1px solid red.

In the following example, the table is wider than the text in any cell, the text in each cell is centered, and the table border is applied to header cells:

```
<html>
<head>
<title>Figure 7-2: Tables</title>
<style>
  table {
    width: 700px;
  }

  table, td {
    text-align: center;
    border: 1px solid black;
    border-collapse: collapse;
  }

</style>
</head>
<body>
 <SPiTable>
    <caption>Desktop browser market share (August 2014)</caption>
    <tr>
      <th>Source</th>
      <th>Chrome</th>
      <th>IE</th>
```

```
        <th>Firefox</th>
        <th>Safari</th>
        <th>Other</th>
      </tr>
      <tr>
        <td>StatCounter</td>
        <td>50%</td>
        <td>22%</td>
        <td>19%</td>
        <td>5%</td>
        <td>4%</td>
      </tr>
      <tr>
        <td>W3Counter</td>
        <td>38%</td>
        <td>21%</td>
        <td>16%</td>
        <td>16%</td>
        <td>9%</td>
      </tr>
    </table>
  </body>
</html>
```

TIP

The HTML tag `<caption>` and the CSS property `border-collapse` further style the table below. The `<caption>` tag adds a title to the table. Although you can create a similar effect using the `<h1>` tag, `<caption>` associates the title with the table. The CSS `border-collapse` property can have a value of `separate` or `collapse`. The `separate` value renders each border separately (refer to Figure 5-9), whereas `collapse` draws a single border when possible (see Figure 7-3).

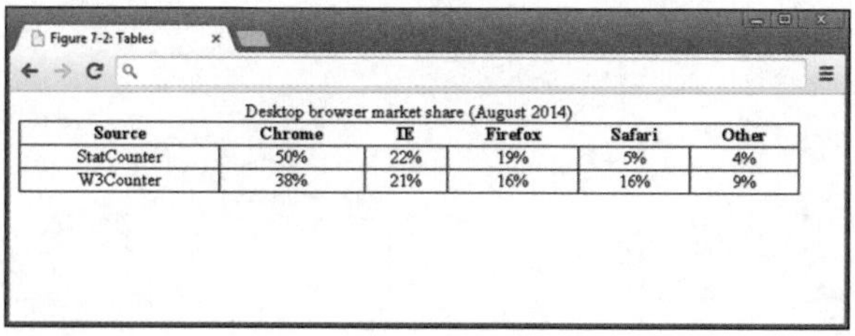

FIGURE 7-3:
Table with width, text alignment, and border modified using CSS.

Figure 7-2: Tables

	Desktop browser market share (August 2014)				
Source	Chrome	IE	Firefox	Safari	Other
StatCounter	50%	22%	19%	5%	4%
W3Counter	38%	21%	16%	16%	9%

Selecting Elements to Style

Currently, the CSS you have seen styles every HTML element that matches the CSS selector. For example, in Figure 7-3 the `table` and `td` selectors have a `text-align` property that centered text in every table cell. Depending on the content, you may want to only center text in the header row, but left-align text in subsequent rows. Two ways to accomplish this include:

>> Styling specific HTML elements based on position to other elements.

>> Naming HTML elements, and only styling elements by name.

Styling specific elements

When styling specific elements, it is helpful to visualize the HTML code as a family tree with parents, children, and siblings. In the following code example (also shown in Figure 7-4, the tree starts with the `html` element, which has two children `head` and `body`. The `head` has a child element called `title`. The `body` has `h1`, `ul`, and `p` elements as children. Finally, the `ul` element has `li` elements as children, and the `p` element has `a` elements as children. Figure 7-4 shows how the following code appears in the browser, and Figure 7-5 shows a depiction of the following code using the tree metaphor. Note that Figure 7-6 shows each relationship once. For example, in the code below there is an `a` element inside each of three `li` elements, and Figure 7-6 shows this `ul` `li` `a` relationship once.

```
<html>
<head>
    <title>Figure 7-3: DOM</title>
</head>
<body>

<h1>Parody Tech Twitter Accounts</h1>
<ul>
    <li>
    <a href="http://twitter.com/BoredElonMusk">Bored Elon Musk</a>
    </li>
    <li>
    <a href="http://twitter.com/VinodColeslaw">Vinod Coleslaw</a>
    </li>
    <li>
    <a href="http://twitter.com/Horse_ebooks">horse ebooks</a>
    </li>
</ul>
```

```
<h1>Parody Non-Tech Twitter Accounts</h1>
<p><a href="http://twitter.com/SeinfeldToday">Modern Seinfeld</a></p>
<p><a href="http://twitter.com/Lord_Voldemort7">Lord_Voldemort7</a></p>

</body>
</html>
```

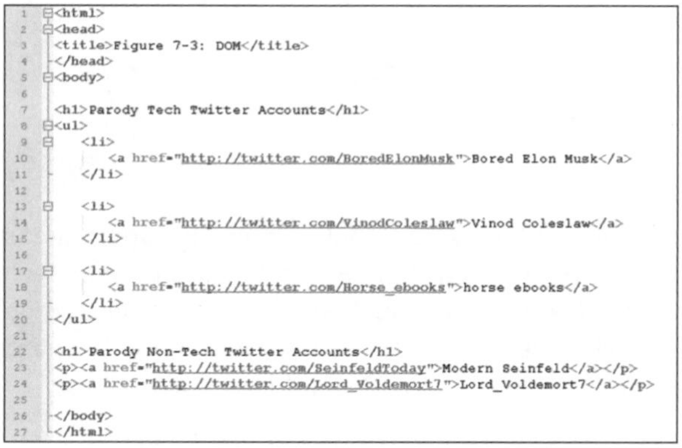

```
1   <html>
2   <head>
3   <title>Figure 7-3: DOM</title>
4   </head>
5   <body>
6
7   <h1>Parody Tech Twitter Accounts</h1>
8   <ul>
9       <li>
10          <a href="http://twitter.com/BoredElonMusk">Bored Elon Musk</a>
11      </li>
12
13      <li>
14          <a href="http://twitter.com/VinodColeslaw">Vinod Coleslaw</a>
15      </li>
16
17      <li>
18          <a href="http://twitter.com/Horse_ebooks">horse ebooks</a>
19      </li>
20  </ul>
21
22  <h1>Parody Non-Tech Twitter Accounts</h1>
23  <p><a href="http://twitter.com/SeinfeldToday">Modern Seinfeld</a></p>
24  <p><a href="http://twitter.com/Lord_Voldemort7">Lord_Voldemort7</a></p>
25
26  </body>
27  </html>
```

FIGURE 7-4:
Styling a family tree of elements.

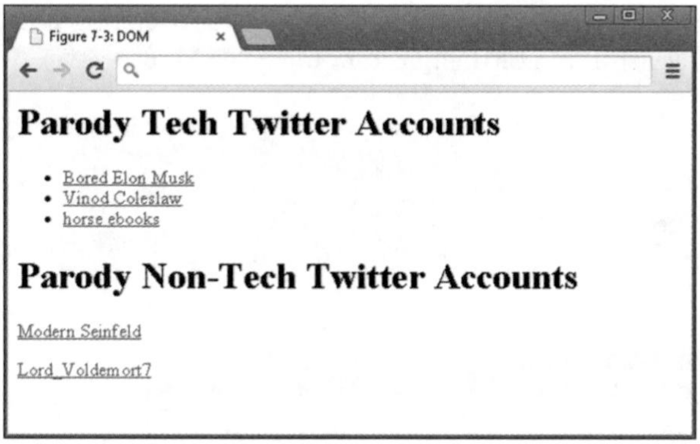

Parody Tech Twitter Accounts

- Bored Elon Musk
- Vinod Coleslaw
- horse ebooks

Parody Non-Tech Twitter Accounts

Modern Seinfeld

Lord_Voldemort7

FIGURE 7-5:
Parody Tech and Non-Tech Twitter accounts (browser view).

TIP

Bored Elon Musk is a parody of Elon Musk, the founder of PayPal, Tesla, and SpaceX. Vinod Coleslaw is a parody of Vinod Khosla, the Sun Microsystems co-founder and venture capitalist. Horse ebooks is a spambot that became an Internet phenomenon.

TECHNICAL STUFF

The HTML tree is called the *DOM* or *document object model*.

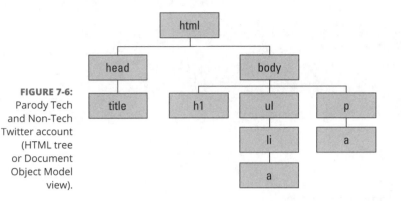

FIGURE 7-6:
Parody Tech and Non-Tech Twitter account (HTML tree or Document Object Model view).

Child selector

The Parody Non-Tech Twitter account anchor tags are immediate children of the paragraph tags. If you wanted to style just the Parody Non-Tech Twitter accounts, you can use the *child selector*, which selects the immediate children of a specified element. A child selector is created by first listing the parent selector, then a greater-than sign (›), and finally the child selector.

In the following example, the anchor tags that are immediate children of the paragraph tags are selected, and those hyperlinks are styled with a red font color and without any underline. The Parody Tech Twitter accounts are not styled because they are direct children of the list item tag. (See Figure 7-7.)

```
p > a {
    color: red;
    text-decoration: none;
}
```

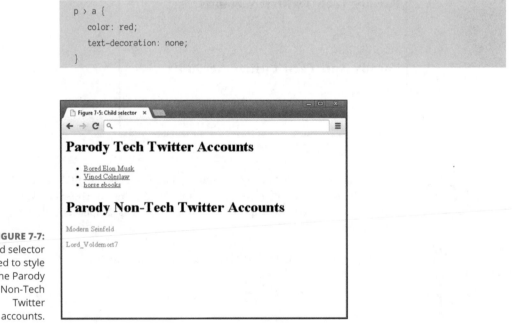

FIGURE 7-7:
Child selector used to style the Parody Non-Tech Twitter accounts.

If you use just the a selector here, all the links on the page would be styled instead of just a selection.

Descendant selector

The Parody Tech Twitter account anchor tags are descendants, or located within, the unordered list. If you wanted to style just the Parody Tech Twitter accounts, you can use the *descendant selector*, which selects not just immediate children of a specified element but all elements nested within the specified element. A descendant selector is created by first listing the parent selector, a space, and finally the descendant selector you want to target.

In the following example, as shown in Figure 7-8, the anchor tags which are descendants of the unordered list are selected, and those hyperlinks are styled with a blue font color and are crossed out. The Parody Non-Tech Twitter accounts are not styled because they are not descendants of an unordered list.

```
ul a {
    color: blue;
    text-decoration: line-through;
}
```

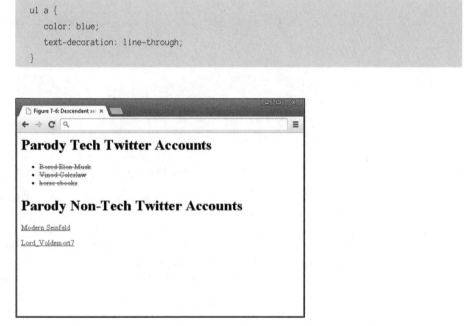

FIGURE 7-8: Child selector used to style the Parody Tech Twitter accounts.

TIP

Interested in styling just the first anchor tag within a list, like the Modern Seinfeld Twitter account, or the second list item, like the Vinod Coleslaw Twitter account? Go to w3schools.com and read more about the first-child (www.w3schools.com/cssref/sel_firstchild.asp), and nth-child selectors (www.w3schools.com/cssref/sel_nth-child.asp).

Naming HTML elements

The other way of styling specific elements in CSS is to name your HTML elements. You name your code by using either the id or class attribute, and then style your code by referring to the id or class selector.

Naming your code using the `id` attribute

Use the id attribute to style one specific element on your web page. The id attribute can name any HTML element, and is always placed in the opening HTML tag. Additionally, each element can have only one id attribute value, and the attribute value must appear only once within the HTML file. After you define the attribute in the HTML file, you refer to the HTML element in your CSS by writing a hashtag (#) followed by the attribute value. Using the id attribute, the following code styles the Modern Seinfeld Twitter link the color red with a yellow background:

HTML:

```
<p><a href="http://twitter.com/SeinfeldToday" id="jerry">Modern Seinfeld</a></p>
```

CSS:

```
#jerry {
   color: red;
   background-color: yellow;
}
```

Naming your code using the `class` attribute

Use the class attribute to style multiple elements on your web page. The class attribute can name any HTML element, and is always placed in the opening HTML tag. The attribute value need not be unique within the HTML file. After you define the attribute in the HTML file, you refer to the HTML element by writing a period (.) followed by the attribute value. Using the class attribute, the following code styles all the Parody Tech Twitter account links the color red with no underline:

HTML:

```
<ul>
   <li>
   <a href="http://twitter.com/BoredElonMusk" class="tech">Bored Elon Musk</a>
   </li>
   <li>
   <a href="http://twitter.com/VinodColeslaw" class="tech">Vinod Coleslaw</a>
   </li>
```

```
    <li>
    <a href="http://twitter.com/Horse_ebooks" class="tech">Horse ebooks</a>
    </li>
</ul>
```

CSS:

```
.tech {
    color: red;
    text-decoration: none;
}
```

TIP

Proactively use a search engine, such as Google, to search for additional CSS effects. For example, if you wanted to increase the spacing between each list item, open your browser and search for *list item line spacing css*. Links appearing in the top ten results should include:

>> www.w3schools.com: A beginner tutorial site.

>> www.stackoverflow.com: A discussion board for experienced developers.

>> www.mozilla.org: A reference guide initially created by the foundation that maintains the Firefox browser, and now maintained by a community of developers.

Each of these sites is a good first place to start, and you should look for answers that include example code.

Aligning and Laying Out Your Elements

CSS not only allows control over the formatting of HTML elements, it also allows control over the placement of these elements on the page, known as page layout. Historically, developers used HTML tables to create page layouts. HTML table page layouts were tedious to create, and required that developers write a great deal of code to ensure consistency across browsers. CSS eliminated the need to use tables to create layouts, helped reduce code bloat, and increased control of page layouts.

Organizing data on the page

Before diving in to any code, let's review in Figure 7-9 some of the basic ways we can structure the page and the content on it. Layouts have evolved over time, with some layouts working well on desktop computers but not displaying optimally on tablet or mobile devices.

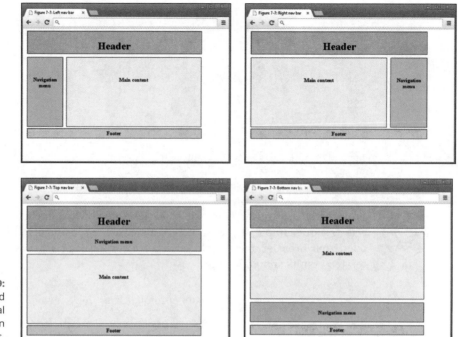

FIGURE 7-9:
Vertical and
horizontal
navigation
layouts.

TIP

Always ask yourself how your intended layout will appear on desktop, tablet, and mobile devices.

Hundreds of different layouts exist, and a few selected page layouts appear here along with example websites:

TIP

Left and right navigation toolbars are not usually seen on mobile devices. Top navigation toolbars are used both on desktop and mobile devices, and bottom navigation toolbars are most common on mobile devices.

The examples in Figure 7-10 show real websites with these layouts:

FIGURE 7-10:
Use of left and
right naviga-
tion toolbar
on w3schools.
com (left) and
hunterwalk.
com (right).

Vertical navigation aids reader understanding when hierarchy or relationship exists between navigational topics. In the w3schools.com example, HTML, Java-Script, Server Side, and XML relate to one another, and underneath each topic heading are related sub-topics.

Horizontal or menu navigation, as shown in Figure 7-11, helps reader navigation with weak or disparate relationships between navigational topics. In the eBay example, the Motors, Fashion, and Electronics menu items have different products and appeal to different audiences.

FIGURE 7-11:
Use of top and bottom navigation toolbar on ebay.com (left) and moma.org (right).

TIP

Don't spend too much time worrying about what layout to pick. You can always pick one, observe whether your visitors can navigate your website quickly and easily, and change the layout if necessary.

Shaping the div

The page layouts above are collections of elements grouped together. These elements are grouped together using rectangular containers created with an opening and closing ⟨div⟩ tag, and all of the layouts above can be created with these ⟨div⟩ tags. By itself, the ⟨div⟩ tag does not render anything on the screen, but instead serves as a container for content of any type like HTML headings, lists, tables, or images. To see the ⟨div⟩ tag in action, take a look at the Codecademy.com home page in Figure 7-12.

Notice how the page can be divided into three parts — the navigation header, the middle video testimonial, and then additional text user testimonials. ⟨div⟩ tags are used to outline these major content areas, and additional nested ⟨div⟩ tags within each part are used to group content like images and text.

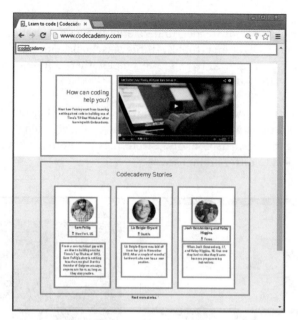

FIGURE 7-12:
Codecademy.
com homepage
with visible
borders for the
`<div>` tags.

In the following example, as shown in Figure 7-13, HTML code is used to create two containers using `<div>` tags, the id attribute names each div, and CSS sizes and colors the div:

HTML:

```
<div id="first"/></div>
<div id="second"/></div>
```

CSS:

```
div {
    height: 100px;
    width: 100px;
    border: 2px solid purple;
}

#first {
    background-color: red;
}

#second {
    background-color: blue;
}
```

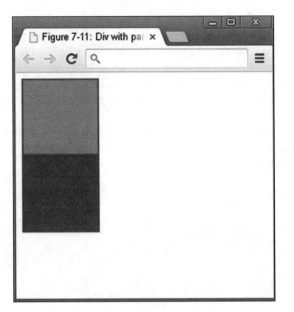

FIGURE 7-13
Two boxes
created with
HTML <DIV>
tag and styled
using CSS.

Understanding the box model

Just as we created boxes with the <div> tags above, CSS creates a box around each and every single element on the page, even text. Figure 7-14 shows the box model for an image that says "This is an element." These boxes may not always be visible, but are comprised of four parts:

» **content:** HTML tag that is rendered in the browser

» **padding:** Optional spacing between content and the border

» **border:** Marks the edge of the padding, and varies in width and visibility

» **margin:** Transparent optional spacing surrounding the border

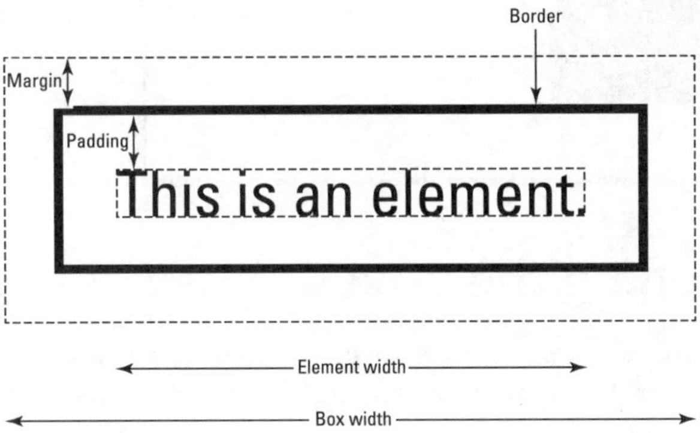

Border

Margin

Padding

This is an element.

Element width

Box width

FIGURE 7-14:
Box model for
img element.

Using the Chrome browser, navigate to your favorite news website, then right-click an image and in the context menu choose Inspect Element. On the right side of the screen you see three tabs; click the Computed tab. The box model is displayed for the image you right-clicked, showing the content dimensions, and then dimensions for the padding, border, and margin.

The padding, border, and margin are CSS properties, and the value is usually expressed in pixels. In the following code, shown in Figure 7-15, padding and margins are added to separate each div.

```css
div {
    height: 100px;
    width: 100px;
    border: 1px solid black;
    padding: 10px;
    margin: 10px;
}
```

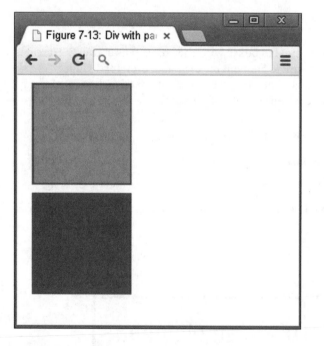

FIGURE 7-15
Padding and margin added to separate each DIV.

Positioning the boxes

Now that you understand how to group elements using HTML, and how CSS views elements, the final piece is to position these elements on the page. Various techniques can be used for page layouts, and a comprehensive overview of each technique is out of the scope of this book. However, one technique to create the layouts shown in Figure 7-16 is to use the `float` and `clear` properties (as described in Table 7-3).

TABLE 7-3   Select CSS Properties and Values for Page Layouts

Property Name	Possible Values	Description
float	left right none	Sends an element to the `left` or `right` of the container it is in. The none value specifies the element should not float.
clear	left right both none	Specifies which side of an element to not have other floating elements.

If the width of an element is specified, the `float` property allows elements that would normally appear on separate lines to appear next to each other, such as navigation toolbars and a main content window. The `clear` property is used to prevent any other elements from floating on one or both sides of current element, and the property is commonly set to `both` to place web page footers below other elements.

The following example code uses ‹div› tags, `float`, and `clear` to create a simple left navigation layout. (See Figure 7-16.) Typically, after grouping your content using ‹div› tags, you name each ‹div› tag using `class` or `id` attributes, and then style the `div` in CSS. There is a lot of code below, so let's break it down into pieces:

>> The CSS is embedded between the opening and closing ‹style› tag, and the HTML is between the opening and closing ‹body› tags.

>> Between the opening and closing ‹body› tag, using ‹div› tags, the page is divided into four parts with header, navigation bar, content, and footer.

>> The navigation menu is created with an unordered list, which is left-aligned, with no marker.

>> CSS styles size, color, and align each ‹div› tag.

>> CSS properties, `float`, and `clear`, are used to place the left navigation layout to the left, and the footer below the other elements.

```
<!DOCTYPE html>
<html>
<head>
 <title>Figure 7-14: Layout</title>
 <style>
   #header{
     background-color: #FF8C8C;
     border: 1px solid black;
     padding: 5px;
     margin: 5px;
     text-align: center;
   }

   #navbar {
     background-color: #00E0FF;
     height: 200px;
     width: 100px;
     float: left;
     border: 1px solid black;
     padding: 5px;
     margin: 5px;
     text-align: left;
   }

   #content {
     background-color: #EEEEEE;
     height: 200px;
     width: 412px;
     float: left;
     border: 1px solid black;
     padding: 5px;
     margin: 5px;
     text-align: center;
   }

   #footer{
     background-color: #FFBD47;
     clear: both;
     text-align: center;
     border: 1px solid black;
     padding: 5px;
     margin: 5px;
   }
```

```
    ul {
      list-style-type: none;
      line-height: 25px;
      padding: 0px;
    }

  </style>
  </head>
  <body>
  <div id="header"><h1>Nik's Tapas Restaurant</h1></div>
```

```
<div id="navbar">
 <ul>
   <li>About us</li>
   <li>Reservations</li>
   <li>Menus</li>
   <li>Gallery</li>
   <li>Events</li>
   <li>Catering</li>
   <li>Press</li>
 </ul>
</div>

<div id="content"><img src="food.jpg" alt="Nik's Tapas"></div>

<div id="footer">Copyright &copy; Nik's Tapas</div>
</body>
</html>
```

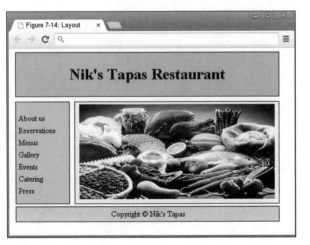

FIGURE 7-16:
Left navigation web page layout created using `<div>` tags.

Writing More Advanced CSS

Practice your CSS online using the Codecademy website. Codecademy is a free website created in 2011 to allow anyone to learn how to code right in the browser, without installing or downloading any software. Practice all of the tags (and a few more) that you learned in this chapter by following these steps:

1. **Open your browser, go to** www.dummies.com/go/codingfd, **and click on the Codecademy link.**

2. **Sign in to your Codecademy account.**

   Signing up is discussed in Chapter 3. Creating an account allows you to save your progress as you work, but it's optional.

3. **Navigate to and click on CSS: An Overview, CSS Selectors, and CSS Positioning to practice CSS styling and positioning.**

4. **Background information is presented in the upper left portion of the site, and instructions are presented in the lower left portion of the site.**

5. **Complete the instructions in the main coding window. As you type, a live preview of your code is generated.**

6. **After you have finished completing the instructions, click the Save and Submit Code button.**

   If you have followed the instructions correctly, a green checkmark appears, and you proceed to the next exercise. If an error exists in your code a warning appears with a suggested fix. If you run into a problem, or have a bug you cannot fix, click on the hint, use the Q&A Forums, or tweet me at @nikhilgabraham and include hashtag #codingFD.

Chapter 8

Working Faster with Twitter Bootstrap

Speed, it seems to me, provides the one genuinely modern pleasure.
—ALDOUS HUXLEY

Twitter Bootstrap is a free toolkit that allows users to create web pages quickly and with great consistency. In 2011, two Twitter developers, Mark Otto and Jacob Thornton, created the toolkit for internal use at Twitter, and soon after released it to the general public. Before Bootstrap, developers would create common web page features over and over again and each time slightly differently, leading to increased time spent on maintenance. Bootstrap has become one of the most popular tools used in creating websites, and is used by NASA and Newsweek for their websites. With a basic understanding of HTML and CSS, you can use and customize Bootstrap layouts and elements for your own projects.

In this chapter, you discover what Bootstrap does and how to use it. You also discover the various layouts and elements that you can quickly and easily create when using Bootstrap.

Figuring Out What Bootstrap Does

Imagine you are the online layout developer for *The Washington Post*, responsible for coding the front page of the print newspaper (see Figure 8-1) into a digital website version. The newspaper consistently uses the same font size and typeface for the main headline, captions, and bylines. Similarly, there are a set number of layouts to choose from, usually with the main headline at the top of the page accompanied by a photo.

FIGURE 8-1: The front page of *The Washington Post* (June 7, 2013).

Every day you could write your CSS code from scratch, defining font typeface, sizes, paragraph layouts, and the like. However, given that the newspaper follows a largely defined format, it would be easier to define this styling ahead of time in your CSS file with class names, and when necessary refer to the styling you want by name. At its core, this is how Bootstrap functions.

Bootstrap is a collection of standardized prewritten HTML, CSS, and JavaScript code that you can reference using class names (for a refresher, see Chapter 7) and then further customize. Bootstrap allows you to create and gives you:

>> **Layouts:** Define your web page content and elements in a grid pattern.

>> **Components:** Use existing buttons, menus, and icons that have been tested on hundreds of millions of users.

>> **Responsiveness:** A fancy word for whether your site will work on mobile phones and tablets in addition to desktop computers. Ordinarily, you would write additional code so your website appears properly on these different screen sizes, but Bootstrap code is already optimized to do this for you, as shown in Figure 8-2.

>> **Cross-browser compatibility:** Chrome, Firefox, Safari, Internet Explorer, and other browsers all vary in the way they render certain HTML elements and CSS properties. Bootstrap code is optimized so your web page appears consistently no matter the browser used.

FIGURE 8-2:
The Angry Birds Star Wars page optimized for desktop, tablet, and mobile using Bootstrap.

Installing Bootstrap

Install and add Bootstrap to your HTML file by following these two steps:

1. Include this line of code between your opening and closing <head> tag:

```
<link rel="stylesheet" href="http://maxcdn.bootstrapcdn.com/
        bootstrap/3.2.0/css/bootstrap.min.css">
```

TIP

The `<link>` tag refers to version 3.2.0 of the Bootstrap CSS file hosted on the Internet, so you must be connected to the Internet for this method to work.

2. **Include both these lines of code immediately before your closing HTML </body> tag.**

```
<!--jQuery (needed for Bootstrap's JavaScript plugins) -->
<script src="http://ajax.googleapis.com/ajax/libs/jquery/1.11.1/jquery.min.
        js"></script>
<!--Bootstrap Javascript plugin file -->
<script src="http://maxcdn.bootstrapcdn.com/bootstrap/3.2.0/js/bootstrap.
        min.js"></script>
```

The first `<script>` tag references a JavaScript library called jQuery. JavaScript is covered in Chapter 9. Although jQuery is not covered in this book, at a high level, jQuery simplifies tasks performed using JavaScript. The second `<script>` tag references Bootstrap JavaScript plugins, including animated effects such as drop-down menus. If your website does not use any animated effects or Bootstrap JavaScript plugins, you don't need to include this file.

Bootstrap is free to use for personal and commercial purposes, but does require including the Bootstrap license and copyright notice.

If you will not have reliable access to an Internet connection, you can also download and locally host the Bootstrap CSS and JavaScript files. To do this, after unzipping the Bootstrap file, use the `<link>` and `<script>` tags to link to the local version of your file. Visit www.getbootstrap.com/getting-started/ to download the files, and to access additional instructions and examples.

Understanding the Layout Options

Bootstrap allows you to quickly and easily lay out content on the page using a grid system. You have three options when using this grid system:

>> **Code yourself:** After you learn how the grid is organized, you can write code to create any layout you wish.

>> **Code with a Bootstrap editor:** Instead of writing code in a text editor, drag and drop components and elements to generate Bootstrap code. You can then download and use this code.

>> **Code with a prebuilt theme:** Download free Bootstrap themes or buy a theme where the website has already been created, and you fill in your own content.

Lining up on the grid system

Bootstrap divides the screen into a grid system of 12 equally-sized columns. These columns follow a few rules:

- » **Columns must sum to a width of 12 columns.** You can use one column that is 12 columns wide, 12 columns that are each one column wide, or anything in between.

- » **Columns can contain content or spaces.** For example, you could have a 4-column-wide column, a space of 4 columns, and another 4-column-wide column.

- » **Unless you specify otherwise, these columns will automatically stack into a single column on smaller browser sizes or screens like mobile devices, and expand horizontally on larger browser sizes or screens like laptop and desktop screens.** See Figure 8-3.

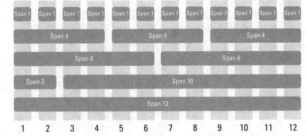

FIGURE 8-3: Sample Bootstrap layouts.

Now that you have a sense for how these layouts appear on the screen, let us take a look at example code used to generate these layouts. To create any layout, follow these steps:

1. **Create a <div> tag with the attribute class="container".**

2. **Inside the first <div> tag, create another nested <div> tag with the attribute class="row".**

3. **For each row you want to create, create another <div> tag with the attribute class="col-md-X". Set X equal to the number of columns you want the row to span.**

   For example, to have a row span 4 columns, write <div class= "col-md-4">. The md targets the column width for desktops, and I show you how to target other devices later in this section.

WARNING

You must include `<div class="container">` at the beginning of your page, and have a closing `</div>` tag or your page will not render properly.

The following code, as shown in Figure 8-4, creates a simple three-column centered layout:

```
<div class="container">
<!-- Example row of columns -->
<div class="row">
 <div class="col-md-4">
   <h2>Heading</h2>
   <p>Lorem ipsum dolor sit amet, consectetur adipisicing elit, sed do eiusmod tempor
         incididunt ut labore et dolore magna aliqua. Ut enim ad minim veniam, quis
         nostrud exercitation ullamco laboris nisi ut aliquip ex ea commodo consequat.
   </p>
 </div>
 <div class="col-md-4">
   <h2>Heading</h2>
   <p>Lorem ipsum dolor sit amet, consectetur adipisicing elit, sed do eiusmod tempor
         incididunt ut labore et dolore magna aliqua. Ut enim ad minim veniam, quis
         nostrud exercitation ullamco laboris nisi ut aliquip ex ea commodo consequat.
   </p>
 </div>
 <div class="col-md-4">
   <h2>Heading</h2>
   <p>Lorem ipsum dolor sit amet, consectetur adipisicing elit, sed do eiusmod tempor
         incididunt ut labore et dolore magna aliqua. Ut enim ad minim veniam, quis
         nostrud exercitation ullamco laboris nisi ut aliquip ex ea commodo consequat.
   </p>
 </div>
</div>
</div>
```

FIGURE 8-4:
Bootstrap three-column layout with desktop (left) and mobile (right) versions.

To see another example, go to the Codecademy site, and resize the browser window. You will notice that as you make the browser window smaller, the columns will automatically stack on top on one another to be readable. Also, the columns are automatically centered. Without Bootstrap, you would need more code to achieve these same effects.

The Lorem ipsum text you see above is commonly used to create filler text. Although the words don't mean anything, the quotation originates from a first-century BC Latin text by Cicero. You can generate filler text when creating your own websites by using www.lipsum.org or www.socialgoodipsum.com.

Dragging and dropping to a website

After looking at the code above, you may want an even easier way to generate the code without having to type it yourself. Bootstrap editors allow you to drag and drop components to create a layout, and after which the editor will generate Bootstrap code for your use.

Bootstrap editors you can use include the following:

>> **Layoutit.com:** Free online Bootstrap editor (as shown in Figure 8-5) that allows you to drag and drop components and then download the source code.

>> **Jetstrap.com:** Paid online drag and drop Bootstrap editor.

>> **Pingendo.com:** Free downloadable drag and drop Bootstrap editor.

>> **Bootply.com:** Free online Bootstrap editor with built-in templates to modify.

FIGURE 8-5: Layoutit.com interface with drag and drop Bootstrap components.

TIP

These sites are free, and may stop working without notice. You can find additional options by using any search engine to search for *Bootstrap editors*.

Using predefined templates

Sites exist with ready-to-use Bootstrap themes; all you need to do is add your own content. Of course, you can also modify the theme if you wish. Some of these Bootstrap theme websites are:

- >> Blacktie.co: Free Bootstrap themes (shown in Figure 8-6), all created by one designer.

- >> Bootstrapzero.com: Collection of free, open-source Bootstrap templates.

- >> Bootswatch.com **and** bootsnipp.com: Includes pre-built Bootstrap components that you can assemble for your own site.

- >> Wrapbootstrap.com: Bootstrap templates available for purchase.

TIP

Bootstrap themes may be available for free, but follow the licensing terms. The author may require attribution, email registration, or a tweet.

FIGURE 8-6:
One page Bootstrap template from blacktie.co.

Adapting layout for mobile, tablet, and desktop

On smaller screens Bootstrap will automatically stack the columns you create for your website. However, you can exercise more control than just relying on the default behavior over how these columns appear. There are four device screen sizes you can target — phones, tablets, desktops, and large desktops. As shown in Table 8-1, Bootstrap uses a different class prefix to target each device.

TABLE 8-1   **Bootstrap Code for Various Screen Sizes**

	Phones (<768 px)	Tablets (≥768px)	Desktops (≥992px)	Large desktops (≥1200 px)
Class prefix	col–sx–	col–sm–	col–md–	col–lg–
Max container width	None (auto)	750px	970px	1170px
Max column width	Auto	~62px	~81px	~97px

Based on Table 8-1, if you wanted your website to have two equal sized columns on tablets, desktops, and large desktops you would use the col–sm– class name as follows:

```
<div class="container">
 <div class="row">
  <div class="col-sm-6">Column 1</div>
  <div class="col-sm-6">Column 2</div>
 </div>
</div>
```

After viewing your code on all three devices, you decide that on desktops you prefer unequal instead of equal columns such that the left column is half the size of the right column. You target desktop devices using the col–md– class name and add it to the class name immediately after col–sm–:

```
<div class="container">
 <div class="row">
  <div class="col-sm-6 col-md-4">Column 1</div>
  <div class="col-sm-6 col-md-8">Column 2</div>
 </div>
</div>
```

TIP

Some elements, such as the <div> tag above, can have multiple classes. This allows you to add multiple effects, such as changing the way a column is displayed, to the element. To define multiple classes, use the class attribute and set it equal to each class; separate each class with a space. For an example, refer to the preceding code: The third <div> element has two classes, col–sm–6 and col–md–4.

Finally, you decide that on large desktop screens you want the left column to be two columns wide. You target large desktop screens using the `col-lg-` class name, as shown in Figure 8-7, and add to your existing class attribute values:

```
<div class="container">
 <div class="row">
  <div class="col-sm-6 col-md-4 col-lg-2">Column 1</div>
  <div class="col-sm-6 col-md-8 col-lg-10">Column 2</div>
 </div>
 </div>
```

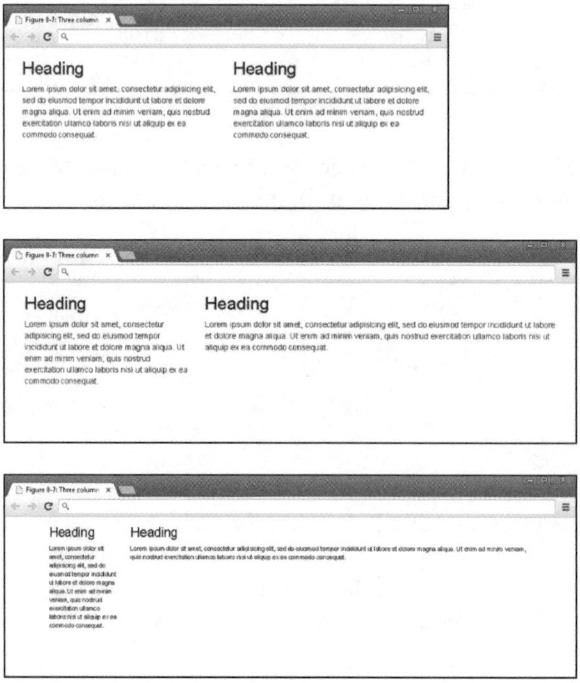

FIGURE 8-7:
A two-column site displayed on tablet, desktop, and large desktop.

Coding Basic Web Page Elements

In addition to pure layouts, Bootstrap can also create web page components found on almost every website. The thought here is the same as when working with layouts — instead of recreating the wheel every time by designing your own button or toolbar, it would be better to use pre-built code, which has already been tested across multiple browsers and devices.

The following examples show how to quickly create common web components.

Designing buttons

Buttons are a basic element on many web pages, but usually can be difficult to set up and style. As shown in Table 8-2, buttons can have various types and sizes.

TABLE 8-2   **Bootstrap Code for Creating Buttons**

Attribute	Class Prefix	Description
Button type	`btn-defaultbtn-primarybtn-successbtn-danger`	Standard button type with hover effect Blue button with hover effect Green button with hover effect Red button with hover effect
Button size	`btn-lgbtn-defaultbtn-sm`	Large button size Default button size Small button size

To create a button, write the following HTML:

>> Begin with the `button` HTML element.

>> In the opening `<button>` tag include `type="button"`.

>> Include the `class` attribute, with the `btn` class attribute value, and add additional class prefixes based on the effect you want. To add additional styles, continue adding the class prefix name into the HTML class attribute.

As shown in Figure 8-8, the following code combines both button type and button size:

```
<p>
  <button type="button" class="btn btn-primary btn-lg">Large primary button</
          button>
  <button type="button" class="btn btn-default btn-lg">Large default
          button</button>
</p>
<p>
  <button type="button" class="btn btn-success">Default Success button</button>
  <button type="button" class="btn btn-default">Default default button</button>
</p>
```

```
<p>
  <button type="button" class="btn btn-danger btn-sm">Small danger
         button</button>
  <button type="button" class="btn btn-default btn-sm">Small default
         button</button>
</p>
```

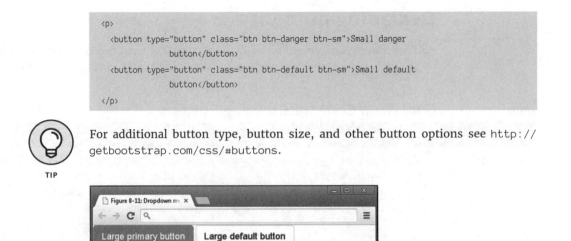

TIP

For additional button type, button size, and other button options see `http://getbootstrap.com/css/#buttons`.

FIGURE 8-8:
Bootstrap
button types
and sizes.

Navigating with toolbars

Web pages with multiple pages or views usually have one or more toolbars to help users with navigation. Some toolbar options are shown in Table 8-3.

TABLE 8-3   **Bootstrap Code for Creating Navigation Toolbars**

Attribute	Class Prefix	Description
Toolbar type	nav-tabs nav-pills	Tabbed navigation toolbar Pill, or solid button navigation toolbar
Toolbar button type	dropdown caret dropdown-menu	Marks button or tab as dropdown menu Down-arrow dropdown menu icon Dropdown menu items

To create a pill or solid button navigation toolbar, write the following HTML:

» Begin an unordered list using the `ul` element.

» In the opening `<ul>` tag, include `class="nav nav-pills"`.

» Create buttons using the `<li>` tag. Include `class="active"` in one opening `<li>` tag to designate which tab on the main toolbar should appear as visually highlighted when the mouse hovers over the button.

» To create a drop-down menu, nest an unordered list. See the code next to "More" with class prefixes "dropdown", "caret", and "dropdown-menu". You can link to other web pages in your drop-down menu by using the `<a>` tag.

The following code, as shown in Figure 8-9, creates a toolbar using Bootstrap:

```
<ul class="nav nav-pills">
  <li class="active"><a href="timeline.html">Timeline</a></li>
  <li><a href="about.html">About</a></li>
  <li><a href="photos.html">Photos</a></li>
  <li><a href="friends.html">Friends</a></li>
  <li class="dropdown">
    <a class="dropdown-toggle" data-toggle="dropdown" href="#">More
    <span class="caret"></span>
    </a>
      <ul class="dropdown-menu">
        <li><a href="places.html">Places</a></li>
        <li><a href="sports.html">Sports</a></li>
        <li><a href="music.html">Music</a></li>
      </ul>
  </li>
</ul>
```

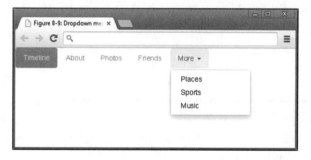

FIGURE 8-9:
Bootstrap toolbar with drop-down menus.

TIP

The `dropdown-toggle` class and the `data-toggle="dropdown"` attribute and value work together to add drop down menus to elements like links. For additional toolbar options, see `http://getbootstrap.com/components/#nav`.

Adding icons

Icons are frequently used with buttons to help convey some type of action. For example, your email program likely uses a button with a trash can icon to delete emails. Icons quickly communicate a suggested action to users without much explanation.

These icons are called *glyphs*, and www.glyphicons.com provides the glyphs used in Bootstrap.

Bootstrap supports more than 200 glyphs, which you can add to buttons or toolbars using the ‹span› tag. As shown in Figure 8-10, the example code below creates three buttons with a star, paperclip, and trash can glyph.

```
<button type="button" class="btn btn-default">Star
  <span class="glyphicon glyphicon-star"></star>
</button>
<button type="button" class="btn btn-default">Attach
  <span class="glyphicon glyphicon-paperclip"></star>
</button>
<button type="button" class="btn btn-default">Trash
  <span class="glyphicon glyphicon-trash"></star>
</button>
```

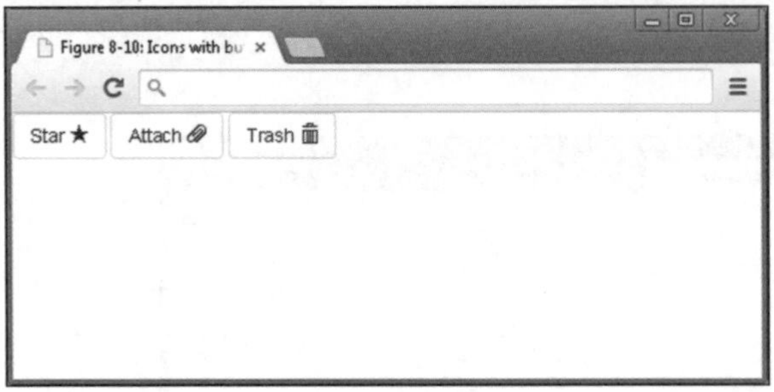

FIGURE 8-10:
Bootstrap buttons with icons

For the names of all the Bootstrap glyphs, see www.getbootstrap.com/components/#glyphicons.

TIP

Build the Airbnb Home Page

Practice Bootstrap online using the Codecademy website. Codecademy is a free website created in 2011 to allow anyone to learn how to code right in the browser, without installing or downloading any software. Practice all of the tags (and a few more) that you learned in this chapter by following these steps:

1. **Open your browser, go to** www.dummies.com/go/codingfd, **and click on the link to Codecademy.**

2. **Sign in to your Codecademy account.**

   Signing up is discussed in Chapter 3. Creating an account allows you to save your progress as you work, but it's optional.

3. **Navigate to and click on Make a Website to practice Bootstrap.**

4. **Background information is presented, and instructions are presented on the site.**

5. **Complete the instructions in the main coding window.**

6. **After you have finished completing the instructions, click the Got It or Save and Submit Code button.**

   If you have followed the instructions correctly, a green checkmark appears and you proceed to the next exercise. If an error exists in your code a warning appears with a suggested fix. If you run into a problem, or have a bug you cannot fix, click on the hint, use the Q&A Forum, or tweet me at @nikhilgabraham and include hashtag #codingFD.

Chapter 9
Adding in JavaScript

The best teacher is very interactive.

—BILL GATES

JavaScript, one of the most popular and versatile programming languages on the Internet, adds interactivity to websites. You have probably seen JavaScript in action and not even realized it, perhaps while clicking buttons that change color, viewing image galleries with thumbnail previews, or analyzing charts that display customized data based on your input. These website features and more can be created and customized using JavaScript.

JavaScript is an extremely powerful programming language, and this entire book could have been devoted to the topic. In this chapter, you learn JavaScript basics, including how to write JavaScript code to perform basic tasks, access data using an API, and program faster using a framework.

What Does JavaScript Do?

JavaScript creates and modifies web page elements, and works with the existing web page HTML and CSS to achieve these effects. When you visit a web page with

JavaScript, your browser downloads the JavaScript code and runs it client-side, on your machine. JavaScript can perform tasks to do any of the following:

>> Control web page appearance and layout by changing HTML attributes and CSS styles.

>> Easily create web page elements like date pickers, as shown in Figure 9-1, and drop-down menus.

>> Take user input in forms, and check for errors before submission.

>> Display and visualize data using complex charts and graphs.

>> Import and analyze data from other websites.

FIGURE 9-1:
JavaScript can create the date picker found on every travel website.

TECHNICAL
STUFF

JavaScript is different from another programming language called Java. In 1996, Brendan Eich, at the time a Netscape engineer, created JavaScript, which was originally called LiveScript. As part of a marketing decision, LiveScript was renamed to JavaScript to try and benefit from the reputation of then-popular Java.

JavaScript was created almost 20 years ago, and the language has continued to evolve since then. In the last decade, its most important innovation has allowed developers to add content to web pages without requiring the user to reload the page. This technique, called *AJAX* (asynchronous JavaScript), probably sounds trivial, but has led to the creation of cutting-edge browser experiences such as Gmail (shown in Figure 9-2).

FIGURE 9-2:
Gmail uses
AJAX, which
lets users
read new
emails without
reloading the
web page.

Before AJAX, the browser would display new data on a web page only after waiting for the entire web page to reload. However, this slowed down the user experience, especially when viewing web pages which had frequent real time updates like web pages with news stories, sports updates, and stock information. JavaScript, specifically AJAX, created a way for your browser to communicate with a server in the background, and to update your current web page with this new information.

TIP

Here is an easy way to think about AJAX: Imagine you are at a coffee shop, and just ordered a coffee after waiting in a really long line. Before asynchronous JavaScript, you had to wait patiently at the coffee bar until you received your coffee before doing anything else. With asynchronous JavaScript, you can read the newspaper, find a table, phone a friend, and do multiple other tasks until the barista calls your name alerting you that your coffee is ready.

Understanding JavaScript Structure

JavaScript has a different structure and format from HTML and CSS. JavaScript allows you to do more than position and style text on a web page — with JavaScript, you can store numbers and text for later use, decide what code to run based on conditions within your program, and even name pieces of your code so you can easily reference them later. As with HTML and CSS, JavaScript has special keywords and syntax that allow the computer to recognize what you are trying to do. Unlike HTML and CSS, however, JavaScript is intolerant of syntax mistakes. If you forget to close an HTML tag, or to include a closing curly brace in CSS, your code may still run and your browser will try its best to display your code. When coding in JavaScript, on the other hand, forgetting a single quote or parenthesis can cause your entire program to fail to run at all.

REMEMBER

HTML applies an effect between opening and closing tags — `<h1>This is a header</strong>`. CSS uses the same HTML element and has properties and values between opening and closing curly braces — `h1 { color: red;}`.

Using Semicolons, Quotes, Parentheses, and Braces

The code below illustrates the common punctuation used in JavaScript — semicolons, quotes, parentheses, and braces (also called curly brackets):

```
var age=22;
var planet="Earth";
if (age>=18)
{
  console.log("You are an adult");
  console.log("You are over 18");

}
else
{
  console.log("You are not an adult");
  console.log("You are not over 18");
}
```

General rules of thumb to know while programming in JavaScript include:

>> Semicolons separate JavaScript statements.

>> Quotes enclose text characters or *strings* (sequences of characters). Any opening quote must have a closing quote.

>> Parentheses are used to modify commands with additional information called *arguments*. Any opening parenthesis must have a closing parenthesis.

>> Braces group JavaScript statements into blocks so they execute together. Any opening brace must have a closing brace.

TIP

These syntax rules can feel arbitrary, and may be difficult to remember initially. With some practice, however, these rules will feel like second nature to you.

Coding Common JavaScript Tasks

JavaScript can be used to perform many tasks, from simple variable assignments to complex data visualizations. The following tasks, here explained within a JavaScript context, are core programming concepts that haven't changed in the last twenty years and won't change in the next twenty. They're applicable to any programming language. Finally, I've listed instructions on how to perform these tasks, but if you prefer you can also practice these skills right away by jumping ahead to the "Writing Your First JavaScript Program" section, later in this chapter.

Storing data with variables

Variables, like those in algebra, are keywords used to store data values for later use. Though the data stored in a variable may change, the variable name remains the same. Think of a variable like a gym locker — what you store in the locker changes, but the locker number always stays the same. The variable name usually starts with a letter, and Table 9-1 lists some types of data JavaScript variables can store.

TABLE 9-1   **Data Stored by a Variable**

Data Type	Description	Examples
Numbers	Positive or negative numbers with or without decimals	156–101.96
Strings	Printable characters	Holly NovakSeñor
Boolean	Value can either be true or false.	truefalse

TECHNICAL STUFF

For a list of rules on variable names see the "JavaScript Variables" section at www.w3schools.com/js/js_variables.asp.

The first time you use a variable name, you use the word var to declare the variable name. Then, you can optionally assign a value to variable using the equals sign. In the following code example, I declare three variables and assign values to those variables:

```
var myName="Nik";
var pizzaCost=10;
var totalCost=pizzaCost * 2;
```

TECHNICAL STUFF

Programmers say you have declared a variable when you first define it using the var keyword. "Declaring" a variable tells the computer to reserve space in memory and to permanently store values using the variable name. View these values by using the console.log statement. For example, after running the preceding example code, running statement console.log(totalCost) returns the value 20.

After declaring a variable, you change its value by referring to just the variable name and using the equals sign, as shown in the following examples:

```
myName="Steve";
pizzaCost=15;
```

TIP

Variable names are case sensitive, so when referring to a variable in your program remember that MyName is a different variable from myname. In general, it's a good idea to give your variable a name that describes the data being stored.

Making decisions with if-else statements

After you have stored data in a variable, it is common to compare the variable's value to other variable values or to a fixed value, and then to make a decision based on the outcome of the comparison. In JavaScript, these comparisons are done using a *conditional statement*. The if-else statement is a type of conditional. Its general syntax is as follows:

```
if (condition) {
    statement1 to execute if condition is true
}
else {
    statement2 to execute if condition is false
}
```

In this statement, the if is followed by a space, and a condition enclosed in parentheses evaluates to true or false. If the condition is true, then statement1, located between the first set of curly brackets, is executed. If the condition is false and if I include the else, which is optional, then statement2, located between the second set of curly brackets, is executed. Note that when the else is not included and the condition is false, the conditional statement simply ends.

TIP

Notice there are no parentheses after the else — the else line has no condition. JavaScript executes the statement after else only when the preceding conditions are false.

The condition in an if-else statement is a comparison of values using operators, and common operators are described in Table 9-2.

TABLE 9-2   # Common JavaScript Operators

Type	Operator	Description	Example
Less than	<	Evaluates whether one value is less than another value	(x < 55)
Greater than	>	Evaluates whether one value is greater than another value	(x > 55)
Equality	===	Evaluates whether two values are equal	(x === 55)
Less than or equal to	<=	Evaluates whether one value is less than or equal to another value	(x <= 55)
Greater than or equal to	>=	Evaluates whether one value is greater than or equal to another value	(x >= 55)
Inequality	!=	Evaluates whether two values are not equal	(x != 55)

Here is a simple `if` statement, without the `else`:

```
var carSpeed=70;
if (carSpeed > 55) {
    alert("You are over the speed limit!");
}
```

In this statement I declare a variable called `carSpeed` and set it equal to 70. Then an `if` statement with a condition compares whether the value in the variable `carSpeed` is greater than 55. If the condition is `true`, an alert, which is a pop-up box, states "You are over the speed limit!" (See Figure 9-3.) In this case, the value of `carSpeed` is 70, which is greater than 55, so the condition is true and the alert is displayed. If the first line of code instead was `var carSpeed=40;` then the condition is false because 40 is less than 55, and no alert would be displayed.

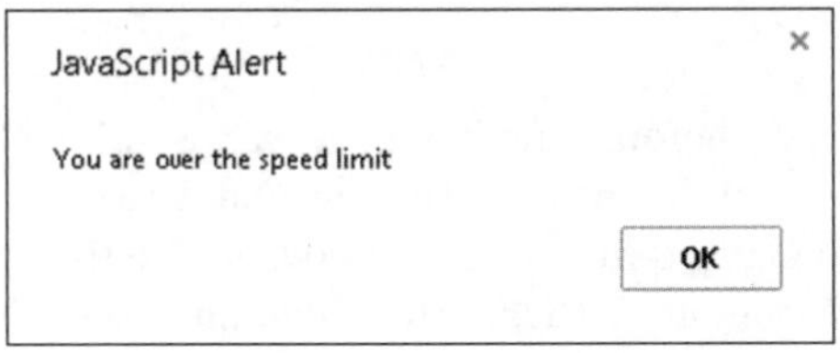

FIGURE 9-3:
The alert
pop-up box.

JavaScript Alert   ×

You are over the speed limit

OK

Let us expand the `if` statement by adding `else` to create an `if-else`, as shown in this code:

```
var carSpeed=40;
if (carSpeed > 55) {
    alert("You are over the speed limit!");
}
else {
    alert("You are under the speed limit!");
}
```

In addition to the `else`, I added an `alert` statement inside the curly brackets following the `else`, and set `carSpeed` equal to 40. When this `if-else` statement executes, `carSpeed` is equal to 40, which is less than 55, so the condition is false, and because the `else` has been added, an alert appears stating "You are under the speed limit!" If the first line of code instead was `var carSpeed=70;` as before, then the condition is true, because 70 is greater than 55, and the first alert would be displayed.

Our current `if-else` statement allows us to test for one condition, and to show different results depending on whether the condition is true or false. To test for two or more conditions, you can add one or more `else if` statements after the original `if` statement. The general syntax for this is as follows:

```
if (condition1) {
    statement1 to execute if condition1 is true
}
else if (condition2) {
    statement2 to execute if condition2 is true
}
else {
    statement3 to execute if all previous conditions are false
}
```

The `if-else` is written as before, and the `else if` is followed by a space, and then a condition enclosed in parentheses that evaluates to either `true` or `false`. If *condition1* is `true`, then `statement1`, located between the first set of curly brackets, is executed. If the *condition1* is `false`, then *condition2* is evaluated and is found to be either `true` or `false`. If *condition2* is `true`, then `statement2`, located between the second set of curly brackets, is executed. At this point, additional `else if` statements could be added to test additional conditions. Only when all `if` and `else if` conditions are `false`, and an `else` is included, is `statement3` executed. Only one statement is executed in a block of code, after which the remaining statements are ignored and the next block of code is executed.

When writing the if–else, you must have one and only one if statement, and, if you so choose, one and only one else statement. The else if is optional, can be used multiple times within a single if–else statement, and must come after the original if statement and before the else. You cannot have an else if or an else by itself, without a preceding if statement.

Here is another example else if statement:

```
var carSpeed=40;
if (carSpeed > 55) {
    alert("You are over the speed limit!");
}
else if (carSpeed === 55) {
    alert("You are at the speed limit!");
}
```

When this if statement executes, carSpeed is equal to 40, which is less than 55, so the condition is false, and then the else if condition is evaluated. The value of carSpeed is not exactly equal to 55 so this condition is also false, and no alert of any kind is shown, and the statement ends. If the first line of code were instead var carSpeed=55; then the first condition is false, because 55 is not greater than 55. Then the else if condition is evaluated, and because 55 is exactly equal to 55, the second alert is displayed, stating "You are at the speed limit!"

Look carefully at the code above — when setting the value of a variable, one equals sign is used, but when comparing whether two values are equal, then three equals signs (===) are used.

As a final example, here is an if–else statement with an else if statement:

```
var carSpeed=40;
if (carSpeed > 55) {
    alert("You are over the speed limit!");
}
else if (carSpeed === 55) {
    alert("You are at the speed limit!");
}
else {
    alert("You are under the speed limit!");
}
```

As the diagram in Figure 9-4 shows, two conditions, which appear in the figure as diamonds, are evaluated in sequence. In this example, the carSpeed is equal to 40, so the two conditions are false, and the statement after the else is executed, showing an alert that says "You are under the speed limit!" Here carSpeed is initially set to 40, but depending on the initial carSpeed variable value, any one of the three alerts could be displayed.

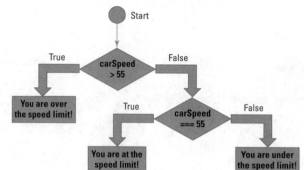

The condition is always evaluated first, and every condition must either be true or false. Independent from the condition is the statement that executes if the condition is true.

REMEMBER

Working with string and number methods

The most basic data types, usually stored in variables, are strings and numbers. Programmers often need to manipulate strings and numbers to perform basic tasks such as the following:

>> Determining the *length* of a string, as for a password.

>> Selecting part (or *substring*) of a string, as when choosing the first name in a string that includes the first and last name.

>> Rounding a number *to fixed* numbers of decimal points, as when taking a subtotal in an online shopping cart, calculating the tax, rounding the tax to two decimal points, and adding the tax to the subtotal.

These tasks are so common that JavaScript includes shortcuts called *methods* (italicized above) that make performing tasks like these easier. The general syntax to perform these tasks is to follow the affected variable's name or value with a period and the name of the method, as follows for values and variables:

```
value.method;
variable.method;
```

Table 9-3 shows examples of JavaScript methods for the basic tasks discussed above. Examples include methods applied to values, such as strings, and to variables.

TABLE 9-3   **Common JavaScript Methods**

Method	Description	Example	Result
`.toFixed(n)`	Rounds a number to *n* decimal places	`var jenny= 8.675309;` `jenny.toFixed(2);`	8.68
`.length`	Represents the number of characters in a string	`"Nik".length;`	3
`.substring (start, end)`	Extracts portion of the string beginning from position `start` to end. Position refers to the location between each character, and starts before the first character with zero.	`var name=` `"Inbox";name.` `substring (2,5);`	box

REMEMBER

When using a string, or assigning a variable to a value that is a string, always enclose the string in quotes.

The `.toFixed` and `.length` methods are relatively straightforward, but the `.substring` method can be a little confusing. The starting and ending positions used in `.substring(start, end)` do not reference actual characters, but instead reference the space between each character. Figure 9-5 shows how the start and end position works. The statement `"Inbox".substring(2,5)` starts at position 2, which is between "n" and "b", and ends at position 5 which is after the "x".

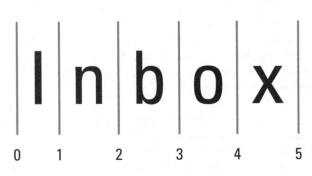

FIGURE 9-5:
The .substring method references positions that are between characters in a string.

TIP

For a list of additional string and number methods see W3Schools `www.w3schools.com/js/js_number_methods.asp` and `www.w3schools.com/js/js_string_methods.asp`.

Alerting users and prompting them for input

Displaying messages to the user and collecting input are the beginnings of the interactivity that JavaScript provides. Although more sophisticated techniques exist today, the `alert()` method and `prompt()` method are easy ways to show a pop-up box with a message, and prompt the user for input.

The syntax for creating an alert or a prompt is to write the method with text in quotes placed inside the parentheses like so:

```
alert("You have mail");
prompt("What do you want for dinner?");
```

Figure 9-6 shows the alert pop-up box created by the `alert()` method, and the prompt for user input created by the `prompt()` method.

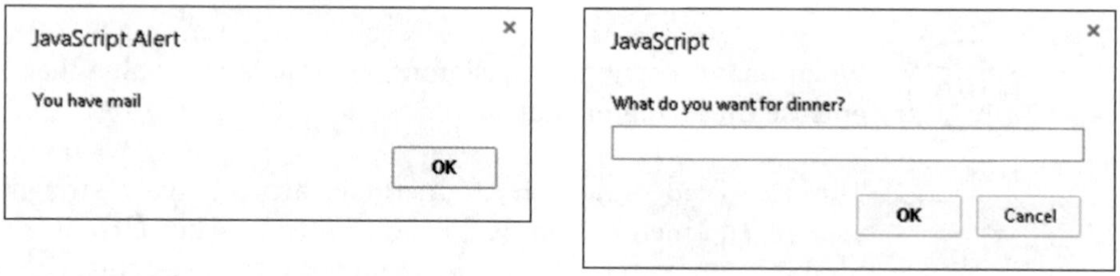

FIGURE 9-6:
A JavaScript alert pop-up box and a user prompt.

Naming code with functions

Functions are a way of grouping JavaScript statements, and naming that group of statements for easy reference with a function name. These statements are typically grouped together because they achieve a specific coding goal. You can use the statements repeatedly by just writing the function name instead of having to write the statements over and over again. Functions prevent repetition and make your code easier to maintain.

When I was younger every Saturday morning my mother would tell me to brush my teeth, fold the laundry, vacuum my room, and mow the lawn. Eventually, my mother tired of repeating the same list over and over again, wrote the list of chores on paper, titled it "Saturday chores," and put it on the fridge. A function names a group of statements, just like "Saturday chores" was the name for my list of chores.

Functions are defined once using the word `function`, followed by a function name, and then a set of statements inside curly brackets. This is called a *function declaration*. The statements in the function are executed only when the function is called by name. In the following example, I have declared a function called greeting that asks for your name using the prompt() method, returns the name you entered storing it in a variable called name, and displays a message with the name variable using the alert() method:

```
function greeting() {
    var name=prompt("What is your name?");
    alert("Welcome to this website " + name);
}


greeting();
greeting();
```

Beneath the function declaration, I have called the function twice, and so I will trigger two prompts for my name, which are stored in the variable name, and two messages welcoming the value in the variable name to this website.

> **TIP**
>
> The "+" operator is used to *concatenate* (combine) strings with other strings, values, or variables.

Functions can take inputs, called *parameters*, to help the function run, and can return a value when the function is complete. After writing my list of chores, each Saturday morning my mother would say "Nik, do the Saturday chores," and when my brother was old enough she would say "Neel, do the Saturday chores." If the list of chores is the function declaration, and "Saturday chores" is the function name, then "Nik" and "Neel" are the parameters. Finally, after I was finished, I would let my mom know the chores were complete, much as a function returns values.

In the following example, I have declared a function called amountdue, which takes price and quantity as parameters. The function, when called, calculates the subtotal, adds the tax due, and then returns the total. The function amount-due(10,3) returns 31.5.

```
function amountdue(price, quantity) {
    var subtotal=price * quantity;
    var tax = 1.05;
    var total = subtotal * tax;
    return total;
}


alert("The amount due is $" + amountdue(10,3));
```

Every opening parenthesis has a closing parenthesis, every opening curly bracket has a closing curly bracket, and every opening double quote has a closing double quote. Can you find all the opening and closing pairs in the example above?

Adding JavaScript to the web page

The two ways to add JavaScript to the web page are:

» Embed JavaScript code in an HTML file using the `script` tag.

» Link to a separate JavaScript file from the HTML file using the `script` tag.

To embed JavaScript code in an HTML file, use an opening and closing ⟨script⟩ tag, and write your JavaScript statements between the two tags, as shown in the following example:

```
<!DOCTYPE html>
<html>
    <head>
        <title>Embedded JavaScript</title>
        <script>
            alert("This is embedded JavaScript");
        </script>
    </head>
<body>
        <h1>Example of embedded JavaScript</h1>
    </body>
</html>
```

TIP

The ⟨script⟩ tag can be placed inside the opening and closing ⟨head⟩ tag, as shown above, or inside the opening and closing ⟨body⟩ tag. There are some performance advantages when choosing one approach over the other, and you can read more at http://stackoverflow.com/questions/436411/where-is-the-best-place-to-put-script-tags-in-html-markup.

The ⟨script⟩ tag is also used when linking to a separate JavaScript file, which is the recommended approach. The ⟨script⟩ tag includes:

» A type attribute, which for JavaScript is always set equal to "text/javascript"

» A src attribute, which is set equal to the location of the JavaScript file.

```
<!DOCTYPE html>
<html>
    <head>
        <title>Linking to a separate JavaScript file</title>
        <script type="text/javascript" src="script.js"/></script>
    </head>
```

```
    <body>
        <h1>Linking to a separate JavaScript file</h1>
    </body>
</html>
```

REMEMBER

The `<script>` tag has an opening and closing tag, whether the code is embedded between the tags or linked to separate file using the `src` attribute.

Writing Your First JavaScript Program

Practice your JavaScript online using the Codecademy website. Codecademy is a free website created in 2011 to allow anyone to learn how to code right in the browser, without installing or downloading any software. Practice all of the tags (and a few more) that you learned in this chapter by following these steps:

1. Open your browser, go to www.dummies.com/go/codingfd, **and click on the link to Codecademy.**

2. Sign in to your Codecademy account.

Signing up is discussed in Chapter 3. Creating an account allows you to save your progress as you work, but it's optional.

3. Navigate to and click on Getting Started with Programming.

4. Background information is presented in the upper left portion of the site, and instructions are presented in the lower left portion of the site.

5. Complete the instructions in the main coding window.

6. After you have finished completing the instructions, click the Save and Submit Code button.

If you have followed the instructions correctly, a green checkmark appears and you proceed to the next exercise. If an error exists in your code a warning appears with a suggested fix. If you run into a problem, or have a bug you cannot fix, click on the hint, use the Q&A Forums, or tweet me at @nikhilgabraham and include hashtag #codingFD.

Working with APIs

Although *APIs* (*application programming interfaces*) have existed for decades, the term has become popular over the last few years as we hear more conversation and promotion around their use. *Use the Facebook API! Why doesn't Craigslist have an API? Stripe's entire business is to allow developers to accept payments online using its payments API.*

Many people use the term API, but few understand its meaning. This section will help clarify what APIs do and how they can be used.

What do APIs do?

An API allows Program A to access select functions of another separate Program B. Program B grants access by allowing Program A to make a data request in a structured, predictable, documented way, and Program B responds to this data request with a structured, predictable, documented response, as follows (see Figure 9-7):

>> It's *structured* because the fields in the request and the data in the response follow an easy-to-read standardized format. For example, the Yahoo Weather API data response includes these selected structured data fields:

```
"location": {
  "city": "New York",
  "region": "NY"
},
"units": {
  "temperature": "F"
},
"forecast": {
    "date": "29 Oct 2014",
    "high": "68",
    "low": "48",
    "text": "PM Showers"
  }
```

TIP

See the full Yahoo Weather API response by visiting http://developer. yahoo.com/weather/.

>> It's *predictable* because the fields that must be included and can be included in the request are pre-specified, and the response to a successful request will always include the same field types.

>> It's *documented* because the API is explained in detail. Any changes usually are communicated through the website, social media, email, and even after the API changes, there is often a period of backward compatibility when the old API requests will receive a response. For example, when Google Maps issued version 3 of their API, version 2 still operated for a certain grace period.

An API allows two separate programs to talk to each other.

Above you saw a weather API response, so what would you include in a request to a weather API? The following fields are likely important to include:

>> Location, which can potentially be specified by using zip code, city and state, current location in latitude and longitude coordinates, or IP address.

>> Relevant time period, which could include the instant, daily, three day, weekly, or 10-day forecast.

>> Units for temperature (Fahrenheit or Celsius) and precipitation (inches or centimeters).

REMEMBER

These fields in our request just specify the desired type and data format. The actual weather data would be sent after the API knows your data preferences.

Can you think of any other factors to consider when making the request? Here is one clue — imagine you work for Al Roker on NBC's *Today* TV show, and you are responsible for updating the weather on the show's website for 1 million visitors each morning. Meanwhile, I have a website, NikWeather, which averages 10 daily visitors who check the weather there. The *Today* website and my website both make a request to the same weather API at the same time. Who should receive their data first? It seems intuitive that the needs of 1 million visitors on the *Today* website should outweigh the needs of my website's 10 visitors. An API can prioritize which request to serve first, when the request includes an API key. An *API key* is a unique value, usually a long alpha-numeric string, which identifies the requestor and is included in the API request. Depending on your agreement with the API provider, your API key can entitle you to receive prioritized responses, additional data, or extra support.

Can you think of any other factors to consider when making the request? Here is another clue — is there any difference in working with weather data versus financial data? The other factor to keep in mind is frequency of data requests and updates. APIs will generally limit the number of times you can request data. In the case of a weather API, maybe the request limit is once every minute. Related to how often you can request the data is how often the data is refreshed. There are two considerations — how often the underlying data changes, and how often the API provider updates the data. For example, except in extreme circumstances the weather generally changes every 15 minutes. Our specific weather API provider may

CHAPTER 9 **Adding in JavaScript** 151

update its weather data every 30 minutes. Therefore, you would only send an API request once every 30 minutes, because sending more frequent requests wouldn't result in updated data. By contrast, financial data such as stock prices and many public APIs, which change multiple times per second, allow one request per second.

Scraping data without an API

In the absence of an API, those who want data from a third-party website create processes to browse the website, search and copy data, and store it for later use. This method of data retrieval is commonly referred to as *screen scraping* or *web scraping*. These processes, which vary in sophistication from simple to complex, include:

» **People manually copying and pasting data from websites into a database:** Crowdsourced websites, such as www.retailmenot.com recently listed on the NASDAQ stock exchange, obtain some data in this way.

» **Code snippets written to find and copy data that match pre-set patterns:** The pre-set patterns are also called *regular expressions*, which match character and string combinations, and can be written using web languages like JavaScript or Python.

» **Automated software tools which allow you to point and click the fields you want to retrieve from a website:** For example, www.kimonolabs.com is one point-and-click solution, and when FIFA World Cup 2014 lacked a structured API, kimonolabs.com extracted data, such as scores, and made it easily accessible.

The advantage of screen scraping is that the data is likely to be available and with less restrictions because it is content that regular users see. If an API fails, it may go unnoticed and depending on the site take time to fix. By contrast, the main website failing is usually a top priority item, and fixed as soon as possible. Additionally, companies may enforce limits on data retrieved from the API that are rarely seen and harder to enforce when screen scraping.

The disadvantage of screen scraping is that the code written to capture data from a website must be precise and can break easily. For example, a stock price is on a web page in the second paragraph, on the third line, and is the fourth word. The screen scraping code is programmed to extract the stock price from that location, but unexpectedly the website changes its layout so the stock price is now in the fifth paragraph. Suddenly, the data is inaccurate. Additionally, there may be legal concerns with extracting data in this way, especially if the website terms and conditions prohibit screen scraping. In one example, Craigslist terms and conditions prohibited data extraction through screen scraping, and after litigation a court banned a company which accessed Craigslist data using this technique.

Researching and choosing an API

For any particular data task there may be multiple APIs that can provide you with the data you seek. The following are some factors to consider when selecting an API for use in your programs:

» **Data availability:** Make a wish list of fields you want to use with the API, and compare it to fields actually offered by various API providers.

» **Data quality:** Benchmark how various API providers gather data, and the frequency with which the data is refreshed.

» **Site reliability:** Measure site uptime because regardless of how good the data may be, the website needs to stay online to provide API data. Site reliability is a major factor in industries like finance and healthcare.

» **Documentation:** Review the API documentation for reading ease and detail so you can easily understand the API features and limitations before you begin.

» **Support:** Call support to see response times and customer support knowledgeability. Something will go wrong and when it does you want to be well supported to quickly diagnose and solve any issues.

» **Cost:** Many APIs provide free access below a certain request threshold. Investigate cost structures if you exceed those levels so you can properly budget for access to your API.

Using JavaScript Libraries

A JavaScript *library* is pre-written JavaScript code that makes the development process easier. The library includes code for common tasks that has already been tested and implemented by others. To use the code for these common tasks, you only need to call the function or method as defined in the library. Two of the most popular JavaScript libraries are jQuery and D3.js.

jQuery

jQuery uses JavaScript code to animate web pages by modifying CSS on the page, and to provide a library of commonly used functions. Although you could write JavaScript code to accomplish any jQuery effect, jQuery's biggest advantage is completing tasks by writing fewer lines of code. As the most popular JavaScript library today, jQuery is used on the majority of top 10,000 most visited websites. Figure 9-8 shows a photo gallery with jQuery transition image effects.

FIGURE 9-8:
Photo gallery
with jQuery
transition
image effects
triggered by
navigation
arrows.

D3.js

D3.js is a JavaScript library for visualizing data. Just like with jQuery, similar effects could be achieved using JavaScript, but only after writing many more lines of code. The library is particularly adept at showing data across multiple dimensions, and creating interactive visualizations of datasets. The creator of D3.js is currently employed at *The New York Times*, which extensively uses D3.js to create charts and graphs for online articles. Figure 9-9 is an interactive chart showing technology company IPO value and performance over time.

FIGURE 9-9:
An IPO chart
showing the
valuation of
the Facebook
IPO relative
to other
technology
IPOs.

Searching for Videos with YouTube's API

Practice accessing APIs using the Codecademy website. Codecademy is a free web-site created in 2011 to allow anyone to learn how to code right in the browser, without installing or downloading any software. Practice all of the tags (and a few more) that you learned in this chapter by following these steps:

1. **Open your browser, go to** www.dummies.com/go/codingfd, **and click on the link to Codecademy.**

2. **Sign in to your Codecademy account.**

   Signing up is discussed in Chapter 3. Creating an account allows you to save your progress as you work, but it's optional.

3. **Navigate to and click on How to use APIs with JavaScript, and then Searching for YouTube Videos.**

4. **Background information is presented in the upper left portion of the site, and instructions are presented in the lower left portion of the site.**

5. **Complete the instructions in the main coding window.**

6. **After you have finished completing the instructions, click the Save and Submit Code button.**

   If you have followed the instructions correctly, a green checkmark appears and you proceed to the next exercise. If an error exists in your code a warning appears with a suggested fix. If you run into a problem, or have a bug you cannot fix, click on the hint, use the Q&A Forums, or tweet me at @nikhilgabraham and include hashtag #codingFD.

3

Putting Together a Web Application

Chapter 10

Building Your Own App

If you have a dream, you can spend a lifetime . . . getting ready for it. What you should be doing is getting started.

—DREW HOUSTON

I f you have read (or skimmed) the previous chapters you now have enough HTML, CSS, and JavaScript knowledge to write your own web application. To review, HTML puts content on the web page, CSS styles that content, and JavaScript allows for interaction with that content.

You may feel like you don't have enough coding knowledge to create an app, but I promise that you do. Besides, the only way to know for certain is to get started and try. In this chapter, you come to better understand the app you are going to build, and the basic steps to create that app. Developers often begin with just the information presented in this chapter and are expected to create a prototype. After reading this chapter think about how you would build the app, and then refer to chapters that follow for more details on each step.

Building a Location-Based Offer App

Technology can provide developers (like you) one of the most valuable pieces of information about your users — their current location. With mobile devices, such as cell phones and tablets, you can even find a user's location when they are on-the-go. Although you likely have used an app to retrieve the time, weather, or even driving directions, you may never have received an offer on your phone to come into a store while walking down the street or driving in a car. Imagine passing by a Mexican restaurant during lunch time and receiving an offer for a free taco. I'm hungry, so let's get started!

Understanding the situation

The following is a fictitious case study. Any resemblance to real companies or events is coincidental.

The McDuck's Corporation is one of the largest fast food restaurants in the world, specializing in selling hamburgers in a restaurant called McDuck's. The company has 35,000 of these restaurants which serve 6.5 million burgers every day to 70 million people in over 100 countries. In September 2014, McDuck's experienced its worst sales decline in over a decade. After many meetings, the executive team decided that the key to improving sales would be increasing restaurant foot traffic. "Our restaurant experience, with burger visuals and french-fry aromas, is the best in the industry — once a customer comes in it is a guaranteed sale," says McDuck's CEO Duck Corleone. To promote restaurant visits, McDuck's wants a web application so customers can check-in to their favorite store, and receive an offer or coupon if they are close to a restaurant. "Giving customers who are 5 or 10 minutes away from a restaurant an extra nudge may result in a visit. Even if customers use this app while at the restaurant, this will allow us to maintain a relationship with them long after they have left," says Corleone.

The McDuck Corporation wants to run a pilot to better understand whether location based offers will increase sales. Your task is to:

>> Create an app that will prove whether location based offers are effective.

>> Limit the app to work on just one McDuck's store of your choice.

>> Obtain the location of customers using the app.

>> Show offers to those customers who are five or ten minutes from the store.

McDuck's currently has a website and a mobile app, but both only show menu and store location information. If this pilot is successful, McDuck's will incorporate your code into its website and mobile app.

Plotting your next steps

Now that you understand McDuck's request, you likely have many questions:

>> What will the app look like?

>> What programming languages will I use to create the app?

>> How will I write code to locate a user's present location?

>> What offer will I show to a user who is 5 to 10 minutes away?

These are natural questions to ask, and to make sure you are asking all the necessary questions upfront in an organized way you will follow a standard development process.

Following an App Development Process

Building an app can take as little time as an hour or as long as decades. For most startups, the development processes for the initial product prototype averages one or two months to complete, whereas enterprise development processes for commercial grade software takes six months to a few years to complete, depending on the industry and the project's complexity. A brief overview of the entire process is described here, and then each step is covered in additional detail as you build the app for McDuck's.

REMEMBER

An app can be a software program that runs on desktop or mobile devices.

The four steps you will follow when building your app are:

>> Planning and discovery of app requirements

>> Researching of technology needed to build the app, and designing the app look and feel

>> Coding your app using a programming language

>> Debugging and testing your code when it behaves differently than you intended

In total, you should plan to spend between two to five hours building this app. As shown in Figure 10-1, planning and research alone will take more than half your time, especially if this is the first time you are building an app. You might be surprised to learn that actually writing code will take a relatively small amount of time, with the rest of your time spent debugging your code to correct syntax and logic errors.

Time Allocations in the App Development Process

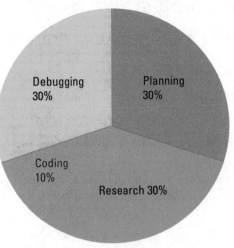

FIGURE 10-1:
Time allocated
to complete
the four steps
in the app
development
process.

App development processes have different names, and the two biggest processes are called *waterfall* and *agile*. Waterfall is a set of sequential steps followed to create a program, whereas agile is a set of iterative steps followed to create a program. Additional discussion can be found in Chapter 3.

TECHNICAL STUFF

Planning Your First Web Application

You or your client has a web app idea, and planning is the process of putting those ideas down on paper. Documenting all the features that will go into the app is so important, because as the cartoon in Figure 10-2 shows for web development, and in computer science generally, it can be difficult to understand upfront what features are technically easy versus difficult to implement.

The planning phase also facilitates an upfront conversation around time, project scope, and budget, where a common saying is to "pick two out of the three." In some situations, such as with projects for finance companies, timelines and project scope may be legally mandated or tied to a big client, and cannot be changed, and so additional budget may need to set aside to meet both. In other situations, such as projects for small startups, resources are scarce so it's more common to adjust the project scope or extend the timeline than to increase the project's budget. Before writing any code, it will be helpful to understand which dimensions can be flexed and which are fixed.

Finally, although you will likely play multiple roles in the creation of this web app, in real life teams of people help bring to life the web apps you use every day. You will see the roles people play, and how everyone works together.

FIGURE 10-2:
It can be difficult to separate technically easy and difficult projects.

Exploring the Overall Process

The purpose of the planning phase is to:

TIP

>> **Understand the client goals:** Some clients may want to be the first to enter an industry with an app, even if it means sacrificing quality. Other clients may require the highest standards of quality, reliability, and stability. Similarly, some others may prioritize retaining existing customers, while others want to attract new customers. All these motivations affect the product design and implementation in big and small ways.

If you are a developer in a large company, your client is usually not the end user but whoever in your internal team must greenlight the app before it is released to the public. At many companies, such as Google, Yahoo, and Facebook, most projects do not pass internal review and are never released to the public.

>> **Document product and feature requests:** Clients usually have an overall product vision, a list of tasks the user must be able to complete with the app. Often, clients have features in mind that would help accomplish those tasks.

>> **Agree on deliverables and a timeline:** Almost every client will imagine a much bigger product than you have time to build. For a developer, it is extremely important to understand what features are absolutely necessary and must be built, and what features are "nice to have" if there is time remaining at the end of the project. If every feature is a "must have" you need to either push the client to prioritize something, or make sure you have given yourself enough time.

TIP

Estimating the time to complete software projects is one of the most difficult project management tasks. There is greater variability and uncertainty than physical construction projects, like building a house, or intellectual projects, like writing a memo. The most experienced developers at the world's best software companies routinely miss estimates, so don't feel bad if completion takes longer than you think. Your estimation skill will improve with time and practice.

After separating the necessary features from the "nice to have," you should decide which features are easy and which are complex. Without previous experience this might seem difficult, but think about whether other applications have similar functionality. You should also try searching the web for forum posts, or products that have the feature. If no product implements the feature, and all online discussion portray the task as difficult it would be worthwhile agreeing up-front on an alternative.

>> **Discuss tools and software you will use to complete the project, and your users will use to consume the project:** Take the time to understand your client and user's workflow to avoid surprises from incompatible software. Web software usually works across a variety of devices, but older operating systems and browsers can cause problems. Defining at the start of the project exactly which browser versions you will support (such as Internet Explorer 9 and later), and which devices (such as desktop and iPhone only) will save development and testing time. Usually, these decisions are based on how many existing users are on those platforms, and many organizations will support a browser version if used by a substantial amount of the user base—usually at least five percent.

TIP

Browser incompatibilities are decreasing as the latest desktop and mobile browsers updates themselves, and are now easier to keep up-to-date.

Meeting the People Who Bring a Web App to Life

You will be able to complete the app in this book by yourself, but the apps you build at work or use every day, like Google Maps or Instagram, are created by teams of people. Teams for a single product can vary in size, reaching upwards of 50 people, and each person plays a specific role across areas like design, development, product management, and testing. In smaller companies, the same person may perform multiple roles, while at larger companies the roles become more specialized and individual people perform each role.

Creating with designers

Before any code has been written, designers work to create the site look and feel through layout, visuals, and interactions. Designers answer simple questions like "should the navigational menu be at the top of the page or the bottom?" to more complex questions like "how can we convey a sense of simplicity, creativity, and playfulness?" In general, designers answer these types of questions by interviewing users, creating many designs of the same product idea, and then making a final decision by choosing one design. Good design can greatly increase adoption of a product or use of site, and products like Apple's iPhone and Airbnb.com. (See Figure 10-3.)

When building a website or app, you may decide you need a designer, but keep in mind within design there are multiple roles that designers play. The following roles are complementary, and may all be done by one person or by separate people:

>> **User interface (UI) and user experience (UX) designers** deal primarily with "look and feel" and with layout. When you browse a website, for example Amazon, you may notice that across all pages the navigation menus, and content are in the same place, and use identical or very similar font, buttons, input boxes, and images. The UI/UX designer thinks about the order in which screens are displayed to the user, along with where and how the user clicks, enters text, and otherwise interacts with the website. If you eavesdropped on UI/UX designers, you may hear conversation like, "his page is too busy with too many call to actions. Our users don't make this many decisions anywhere else on the site. Let's simplify the layout by having just a single Buy button so anyone can order in just one click."

>> **Visual designers** deal primarily with creating the final graphics used on a website, and is the role most closely associated with "designer." The visual designer creates final versions of icons, logos, buttons, typography, images.

For example, look at your Internet browser — the browser icon, the Back, Reload, and Bookmark buttons are all created by a visual designer, and anyone using the browser for the first time will know what the icons mean without explanation. If you eavesdropped on visual designers, you may hear conversation like, "The color contrast on these icons is too light to be readable, and if including text with the icon, let's center-align the text below the icon instead of above it."

>> **Interaction designers** deal primarily with interactions and animations based on user input and situation. Initially, interaction design were limited to keyboard and mouse interactions, but today touch sensors on mobile devices have created many more potential user interactions. The interaction designer thinks about how to use the best interaction so the user is able to complete a task as easily as possible. For example, think about how you check your email on your mobile phone. For many years, the traditional interaction was to see a list of messages, click on a message, and then click on a button to reply, flag, folder, or delete the message. In 2013, interaction designers rethought the email app interaction, and created an interaction so users could swipe their finger left or right to delete or reply to email messages instead of having to click through multiple menus. If you eavesdropped on interaction designers, you may hear conversation like, "While users are navigating with our maps app, instead of letting us know they are lost by clicking or swiping, maybe they can shake the phone and we instantly have a location specialist call them."

TIP

If creating an app was like making a movie, designers would be screenwriters.

FIGURE 10-3: Jonathan Ive, SVP of Design at Apple, is credited for Apple's design successes.

Coding with front- and back-end developers

After the design is complete, the front-end and back-end developers make those designs a reality. Front-end developers, such as Mark Otto and Jacob Thornton (see Figure 10-4), code in HTML, CSS, and JavaScript, and convert the design into a user interface. These developers write the same code that you have been learning throughout this book, and ensure the website looks consistent across devices (desktop, laptop, and mobile), browsers (Chrome, Firefox, Safari, and so on), and operating systems (Windows, Mac, and so on). All these factors, especially increased adoption of mobile device, result in thousands of combinations that must be coded for and tested because every device, browser, and operating system renders HTML and CSS differently.

FIGURE 10-4:
Mark Otto and Jacob Thornton created Bootstrap, the most popular front-end framework.

TIP

If creating an app was like making a movie, front-end developers would be the starring actors.

Back-end developers such as Yukihiro Matsumoto (see Figure 10-5) add functionality to the user interface created by the front-end developers. Back-end developers ensure everything that's not visible to the user and behind the scenes is in place for the product to work as expected. Back-end developers use server-side languages like Python, PHP, and Ruby to add logic around what content to show, when, and to whom. In addition, they use databases to store user data, and create servers to serve all of this code to the users.

TIP

If creating an app was like making a movie, back-end developers would be the cinematographers, stunt coordinators, makeup artists, and set designers.

Managing with product managers

Product managers help define the product to be built, and manage the product development process. When engineering teams are small (such as fifteen people or less) communication, roles, and accountability are easily managed internally without much formal oversight. As engineering teams grows, the overhead of everyone communicating with each other also grows, and without some process can become unmanageable, leading to miscommunication and missed deadlines. Product managers serve to lessen the communication overhead, and when issues arise as products are being built decide whether to extend timelines, cut scope, or add more resources to the team. Product managers are often former engineers, who have a natural advantage in helping solve technical challenges that arise, but non-technical people are also assuming the role with success. Usually, no engineers report to the product manager, causing some to comment that product managers have "all of the responsibility, and none of the authority." One product manager wielding great responsibility and authority is Sundar Pichai, who originally was a product manager for the Google toolbar, and recently was appointed to oversee many of Google's products, including search, Android, Chrome, maps, ads, and Google+. (See Figure 10-6.)

Testing with quality assurance

Testing is the final step of the journey after an app or website has been built. As a result of the many hands that helped with production, the newly created product will inevitably have bugs. Lists are made of all the core app user tasks and flows, and human testers along with automated programs go through the list over and over again on different browsers, devices, and operating systems to find errors. Testers compile the newly discovered bugs, and send them back to the developers, who prioritize which bugs to squash first. Trade-offs are always made between how many users are affected by a bug, the time it takes to fix the bug, and the time left until the product must be released. The most important bugs are fixed immediately, and minor bugs are scheduled to be fixed with updates or later released. Today, companies also rely on feedback systems and collect error reports from users, with feedback forms and in some cases through automated reporting.

Chapter 11

Researching Your First Web Application

If we knew what it was we were doing, it would not be called research.
—ALBERT EINSTEIN

With the basic requirements defined, the next step is researching how to build the application. Apps consist of two main parts: functionality and form (design). For each of these parts, you must:

>> **Divide the app into steps:** Although it's good practice to divide anything you are going to build into steps, diving apps into manageable pieces is an absolute necessity for large software projects with many people working across multiple teams.

>> **Research each step:** When doing your research, the first question to ask is whether you must build a solution yourself or use an existing solution built by someone else. Building your own solution usually is the best way to directly address your need, but it takes time, whereas implementing someone else's solution is fast but may only meet part of your needs.

>> **Choose a solution for each step:** You should have all the solutions selected before writing any code. For each step, decide whether you are writing your own code, or using pre-built code. If you are not writing the code yourself, compare a few options so you can pick one with confidence.

Dividing the App into Steps

The biggest challenge with dividing an app into steps is knowing how big or small to make each step. The key is to make sure each step is discrete and independent. To test whether you have the right number of steps, ask yourself if someone else could solve and complete the step with minimal guidance.

Finding your app's functionality

Recall that McDuck's wants to promote restaurant visits by using a web application that sends customers an offer or coupon if they're close to a restaurant. To make this job easier, you are to create the app for customers visiting just one store.

Your first move is to break down this app into steps needed for the app to function. These steps should not be too specific: Think of them in broad terms, as if you were explaining the process to a kindergartner. With a pen and paper, write down these steps in order. Don't worry about whether each step is correct, as your skill will improve with practice and time. To help you start, here are some clues:

>> Assume the McDuck's app activates when the customer presses a button in the app to check-in to a store.

>> When the button is pressed, what are the two locations that the app must be aware of?

>> When the app is aware of these two locations, what calculation involving these two locations must the computer make?

>> After computing this calculation, what effect will the computer show?

Fill out your list now, and don't continue reading until you've completed it.

Finding your app's functionality: My version

The following is my version of the steps needed to make the app function according to McDuck's specifications. My steps may differ from yours, of course, and this variation is completely fine. The important lesson here is that you understand why each of these steps is necessary for the app to work:

1. **The customer presses a button on the app.**

   The instructions above said to initiate the app with the press of a button. That being said, there are two other options for launching the app:

- *Executing the steps continuously in the background, regularly checking the customer's location.* Currently, this technique places a heavy drain on the battery, and is not usually recommended.

- *Executing the steps only when the customer opens the app.*

2. **After the button is pressed, find the customer's current location.**

The customer's location is one of the two locations you need to identify. The customer's current location is not fixed, and it changes, for example, when the customer is walking or driving.

3. **Find the fixed location of a McDuck's store.**

The McDuck's restaurant location is the other location you need to identify. Because this is a pilot, you only need to identify the location for one McDuck's restaurant, a fixed location that will not change. Hypothetically, assuming that the pilot is successful and that McDuck's wants to implement this app for users visiting all 35,000 restaurants, you'd have to track many more restaurant locations. Additionally, in a larger rollout the locations would need to be updated regularly, as new restaurants open, and as existing restaurants move or close.

4. **Calculate the distance between the customer's current location and the McDuck's restaurant, and name this distance *Customer Distance*.**

This step calculates how far away the customer is from the McDuck's restaurant. One complexity to be aware of—but not to worry about right now—is the direction in which the customer is moving. Although McDuck's did not specify whether they want to display offers to customers heading both toward and away from their store, this may be a question worth asking anyway.

5. **Convert five to ten minutes of customer travel into a distance called *Threshold Distance*.**

McDuck's CEO Duck Corleone wants to target customers who are five to ten minutes away from the store. Distance, in this sense, can be measured in both time and in units of distance such as miles. For consistency, however, plan to convert time into distance—translate those five to ten minutes into miles. The number of miles traveled in this time will vary by common mode of transportation and by location, because five to ten minutes of travel in New York City won't get you as far as five to ten minutes of travel in Houston, Texas.

6. **If the Customer Distance is less than the Threshold Distance, then show an offer to the customer.**

Following McDuck's specifications, the app should attract customers to come to the store, and so the app only shows offers to customers who are close to the restaurant. Another complexity to be aware of—but not to worry about right now—is that the Customer Distance can change quickly. Customers traveling by car could easily be outside the Threshold Distance one minute and inside it the next. Figure 11-1 shows the customers we want to target, relative to a fixed restaurant location.

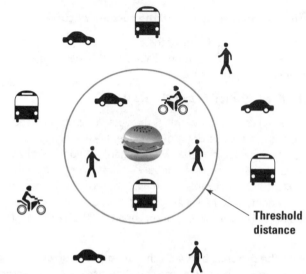

FIGURE 11-1: Customers we want to target based on a fixed restaurant location.

Threshold distance

REMEMBER

Many software logic mistakes happen at this stage, because the programmer forgets to include a step. Take your time reviewing these steps and understanding why each step is essential, and why this list of steps is the minimum necessary to operate the app.

Finding your app's form

After you settle on what the app will do, you must find the best way to present this functionality to users. There are many ways that users can interact with your app's functionality, so picking out the right approach can be tricky. Designing an app can be fun and rewarding, but it's hard work. After the first iteration of an app's design, developers are often disappointed: Users will rarely use the product as intended and will find many parts of the app confusing. This is natural — especially because at this stage you're often creating something or having the user do something that hasn't been done before. Your only choice is to keep trying, to keep testing, modifying, and creating new designs until your app is easy for everyone to use. Although the iPod is a hardware product, the approach Apple took to perfect it is basically the same. Figure 11-2 shows how the design can change over time, with the button layout changing from the original click-wheel to individual horizontal buttons, and finally back to the click-wheel again.

(1st Gen)   (2nd/3rd Gen)   (4th Gen)

FIGURE 11-2:
Apple's iPod
design changes
over multiple
product
releases.

(4th Gen w/Color)   (5th Gen, Video)   (Classic)

The following list describes a basic design process to create the look and feel of your app:

1. **Define the main goals of your app.**

   If you were at a party, and you had to explain what your app did in one sentence, what would it be? Some apps help you hail a taxi, reserve a table at a restaurant, or book a flight. Famously, the goal for the iPod was 1,000 songs in your pocket accessible within three clicks, which helped create an easy to use user interface. An explicitly defined goal will serve as your north star, helping you to resolve questions and forcing you to keep trying.

2. **Break these goals into tasks.**

   Each goal is the sum of many tasks, and listing them will help you design the shortest path to completing each task and ultimately the goal. For instance, if your app's goal is for a user to book a flight, then the app will likely need to record desired flying times and destinations, search and select flights departing during those times, record personal and payment information, present seats for selection, and confirm payment of the flight. Sometimes designers will segment tasks by user persona, another name for the person completing the task. For example, this app may be used by business and leisure travelers. Leisure travelers may need to do heavy searching and pick flights based on price, while business travelers mostly rebook completed flights and pick flights based on schedule.

3. Research the flows and interactions necessary to accomplish these tasks.

For example, our flight app requires the user to select dates and times. One immediate question is whether the date and time should be two separate fields or one field, and on a different or same screen as the destination. Try to sketch what feels intuitive for you, and research how others have solved this problem. You can use Google to find other travel apps, list all the various designs, and either pick or improve upon the design you like best. Figure 11-3 shows two different approaches to flight search. Similarly, you can also use design-centric sites, such as www.dribbble.com, to search designer portfolios for features and commentary.

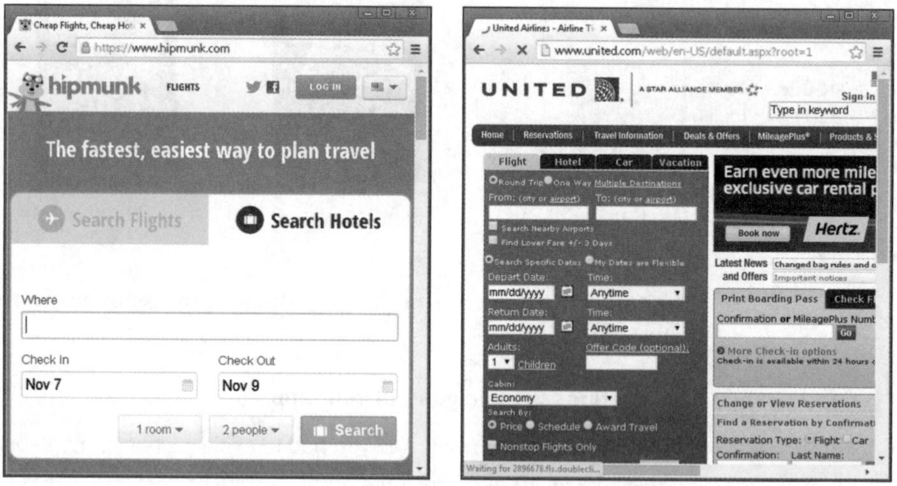

FIGURE 11-3: Different designs for flight reservation from Hipmunk.com and United Airlines.

4. Create basic designs, called *wireframes*, and collect feedback.

Wireframes, as shown in Figure 11-4, are low fidelity website drawings which show structurally how site content and interface interact. Wireframes are simple to create, but should have enough detail to elicit feedback from others. Many wireframe tools use a simple almost pencil-like drawing to help anyone providing comments to focus on the structural and bigger picture design, instead of smaller details like button colors or border thicknesses. Feedback at this stage to refine design is so important because the first wireframe likely does not address users' main concerns and overcomplicates the tasks a user needs to do.

TIP

With mobile devices increasing in popularity relative to desktop devices, remember to create mobile and desktop versions of your wireframes.

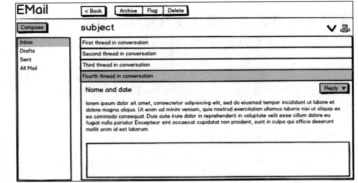

FIGURE 11-4:
A wireframe
for an email
client.

5. Create mock-ups and collect more feedback. (See Figure 11-5.)

After you have finished talking to your client and to users, it is time to create mock-ups, which are high fidelity website previews. These designs have all the details a developer needs to create the website including final layout, colors, images, logos, and sequences of screens to show when the user interacts with the web page. After creating a mock-up, plan to collect more feedback.

FIGURE 11-5:
A mock-up for
an email client.

TIP

Collecting feedback at every stage of the design process might seem unnecessary, but it is much easier to explore different designs and make changes before any code has been written.

6. Send the final file to the developers.

After the mock-up has been created and approved, you typically send a final image file to the developer. Although this file could be in any image file format like PNG or JPG, the most popular file format used by designers is PSD, created using Adobe Photoshop.

Finding your app's form: The McDuck's Offer App design

In this section you follow the design process described in the previous section to create a simple design for the McDuck's Offer app. As part of the design, you should do the following things:

1. **Define the main goals of your app.**

The main goal for McDuck's is to use offers to attract customers to restaurants.

2. **Break these goals into tasks.**

Customers need to view the offer, navigate to the store, and use the offer.

3. **Research the flows and interactions needed to accomplish these tasks.**

Because this is the first iteration of the app, let's focus on just allowing the customer to view the offer.

One function that McDuck's did not specify is the ability to save single-use coupons and to share general-use coupons. However, when looking at other apps, like the ones in Figure 11-6, the need for this becomes more obvious. Also, some similar apps allow the customer to spend money to *buy* coupons—maybe this functionality should be added as well. These questions would be great to present to McDuck's later.

FIGURE 11-6: Example flow from deals and offer apps currently in the market.

The apps in Figure 11-6 also all display various "call to action" buttons to the user before displaying the deal. Some apps ask the user to check-in to a location, other apps ask the user to purchase the coupon, and still others show a collection of new or trending coupons today.

For now, and to keep things simple, let's assume that our McDuck's app has a button that allows customers to check-in to their favorite McDuck's location, and when clicked within the target distance the app displays a general-use coupon that customers receive for free.

4. **Create basic designs, called wireframes, and collect feedback.**

   A sample design for the app, based on the look and feel of other apps, appears in Figure 11-7.

5. **Create mock-ups and collect more feedback.**

   Ordinarily, you would create *mock-ups*, which are more polished designs with real images, from the wireframes and present them to customers for feedback. In this case, however, the app is simple enough that you can just start coding.

Identifying Research Sources

Now that you know *what* your app will do, you can focus on *how* your app will do it. After breaking down your app into steps, you go over each step to determine how to accomplish it. For more complicated apps, developers first decide which of these two methods is the best way to complete each step:

» **Building code from scratch:** This is the best option if the functionality in a particular step is unique or strategically important, an area of strength for the app, and existing solutions are expensive or non-existent. With this option, you and developers within the company write the code.

» **Buying or using a pre-existing solution:** This is the best option if the functionality in a particular step is common, non-core technical area for the app, and existing solutions are competitively priced. With this option, you and developers working on the app use code written by external third party developers.

One company that recently made this decision — publicly and painfully — is Apple with its Maps product. In 2012, after years of using Google Maps on its mobile devices, Apple decided to introduce its own maps application that it had been developing for two years. Although the Maps product Apple built internally turned out to initially be a failure, Apple decided to build its own mapping application because it viewed mapping capabilities as strategically important and because turn-by-turn navigation solutions were not available in the solution provided by Google.

Whether you're building or buying, research is your next step. Here are some sources to consider when researching:

>> **Search engines:** Use Google.com or another search engine to type in what you are trying to accomplish with each step. One challenge can be discovering how the task you're trying to achieve is referred to by programmers. For instance, if I want to find my current location, I might enter *show my location in an app* into a search engine, but this results in a list of location-sharing apps. After reading a few of the top ten results, I see that location-tracking is also referred to as *geolocation*. When I search again for geolocation the top results include many examples of code that shows my current location.

TIP

For more generic searches for code examples, try including the name of the computer language and the word *syntax*. For example, if you want to insert an image on a web page, search for *image html syntax* to find code examples.

>> **Prior commercial and open-source apps:** Examining how others built their apps can give you ideas on how to improve upon what already exists, and insight into pushing existing technology to the limit to achieve an interesting effect. For instance, say you wanted to build a mobile app that recognized TV ads from the "audio fingerprint" of those ads and directed viewers to a product page on a mobile device. To create this app, you could build your own audio fingerprinting technology, which would likely take months or longer to build, or you could partner with Shazam, a commercial application, or Echoprint, an open-source music fingerprinting service. Either app can record a 10 to 20-second audio sample, create a digital fingerprint after overcoming background noise and poor microphone quality, compare the fingerprint to large audio database, and then return identification information for the audio sample.

>> **Industry news and blogs:** Traditional newspapers, like the *Wall Street Journal,* and tech blogs, like TechCrunch.com, report on the latest innovations in technology. Regularly reading or searching through these sites is a good way to find others who have launched apps in your space.

>> **API directories:** You can easily search thousands of APIs for the functionality you need to implement. For example, if you were creating an app that used face recognition instead of a password, you could search for *face detection APIs* and use an API you find instead of trying to build a face detection algorithm from scratch. Popular API directories include www.programmableweb.com and www.mashape.com.

As discussed in Chapter 9, APIs are a way for you to request and receive data from other programs in a structured, predictable, documented way.

>> **User-generated coding websites:** Developers in different companies frequently face the same questions on how to implement functionality for features. Communities of developers online talk about shared problems and contribute code so anyone can see how these problems have been solved in the past. You can participate in developer conversation and see the code other developers have written by using www.stackoverflow.com and www.github.com.

Researching the Steps in the McDuck's Offer App

To implement the functionality in the McDuck's Offer app, you broke down the app into six steps using plain English. Now, research how you can convert those steps into code using the resources listed in the previous section. Your app will require HTML to put content on the page, CSS to style that content, and JavaScript for the more interactive effects. Do your best to research each of the steps on your own, write down the answers, and then look over the suggested code in the next section:

>> **"The customer presses a button on the app:"** This code creates a button that triggers every subsequent step. Creating a button on a web page is a very common task, so to narrow down the results search for *html button tag*. Review some of the links in the top 10 search results, and then write down the HTML tag syntax to create a button that says "McDuck's Check-in."

In your search results, sites like w3schools.com are designed for beginners, and will include example code and simple explanations.

>> **"After the button is pressed, find the customer's current location:"** In web lingo, finding a user's location is called *geolocation*. I will provide you with JavaScript geolocation code, along with an explanation for how it works and where I found it. To trigger this JavaScript code, you need to add an attribute to the HTML button tag to call a JavaScript function named getlocation().

TIP

As described in Chapter 4, HTML attributes are inserted in the opening HTML tag.

Search for *html button javascript button on click* to find out how to insert the onclick attribute to your button HTML code. Review the search results, and then write down the HTML syntax for your button code.

» **"Find the fixed location of a McDuck's store:"** You'll need a real-world address to serve as the McDuck's store. Use a mapping application like maps.google.com to find the street address of a burger restaurant near you. Computers typically represent physical addresses using latitude and longitude numbers instead of street addresses. You can search for websites that convert street addresses into latitude and longitude numbers, or if you're using Google Maps, you can find the numbers in the URL, as shown in Figure 11-8. The first number after the @ sign and up to the comma is the latitude, and the second number between the two commas is the longitude. Figure 11-8 shows a McDonald's store in New York City, and the latitude is 40.7410344, and the longitude is –73.9880763.

Track down the latitude and longitude numbers for the burger restaurant of your choice, up to seven decimal places, and write them down on a piece of paper.

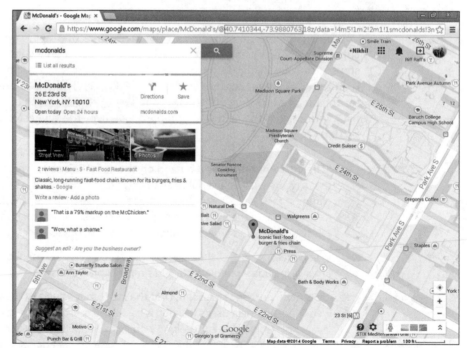

FIGURE 11-8:
Latitude and longitude of a McDonald's in New York City.

Include a negative sign if you see one, and all seven decimal places for the greatest accuracy.

» **"Calculate the distance between the customer's current location and the McDuck's restaurant, and name this distance *Customer Distance*:"** Latitude and longitude are coordinates that represent a location on a sphere. The distance along the surface of the sphere between two sets of latitude and longitude coordinates is calculated using the Haversine formula. You can find a JavaScript version of the formula at stackoverflow.com/ questions/27928/how-do-i-calculate-distance-between-two-latitude-longitude-points. This is the formula you will use to calculate distance when creating the McDuck's app, and I will include this code for you.

Don't get bogged down in the details of how the Haversine formula works. Abstraction is an important concept to remember when programming, and this basically means that as long as you understand the inputs to a system, and the outputs, you don't really need to understand the system itself, much as you don't need to understand the mechanics of the internal combustion engine in order to drive a car.

» **"Convert five to ten minutes of customer travel into a distance called *Threshold Distance*:"** Using the most common method of transportation in your current city, write down the number of miles you could you travel, on average, in five to ten minutes.

» **"If the Customer Distance is less than the Threshold Distance then show an offer to the customer:"** The two pieces to research for this step are the conditional statement that decides when to show the offer to the consumer, and the actual offer:

- *The conditional statement:* This is written in JavaScript using an if-else statement. If the customer is within the threshold distance, then it shows the offer; otherwise (else) it shows another message. To review the if-else syntax, search Google or another search engine for *JavaScript if-else statement syntax* (or refer to Chapter 9 to review the coverage of the if-else statement syntax there).

- *The offer to show to the consumer:* The easiest way to show an offer is to use the JavaScript alert(). Search for *JavaScript alert syntax*.

After you've conducted your searches, write down your if-else statement with a text alert() for a free burger if the customer is within the Threshold Distance, and a text alert() notifying the customer they have checked in.

When you have the if-else statement working, you can replace the text alert() with an image. Search http://images.google.com for a burger coupon image. After you find the image, left-click on it from the image grid in the search results, and left-click again on View Image button. When the image loads the direct link to the image will be in the URL address bar in the browser. The code to insert the image is shown in Chapter 4.

Choosing a Solution for Each Step

With your research finished, it's time to find the best solution. If multiple solutions exist for each step, you now need to choose one. To help you choose, weigh each of your multiple solutions across a variety of factors, such as these:

>> **Functionality:** Will the code you write or pre-built solution you found do everything you need?

>> **Documentation:** Is there documentation for the pre-built solution, like instructions or a manual, that is well written with examples?

>> **Community and support:** If something goes wrong while writing your code, is there a community you can turn to for help? Similarly, does the pre-built solution have support options you can turn to if needed?

>> **Ease of implementation:** Is implementation as simple as copying a few lines of code? Or is a more complex setup or an installation of other supporting software necessary?

>> **Price:** Every solution has a price, whether it is the time spent coding your own solution or the money paid for someone else's pre-built code. Think carefully about whether your time or money is more important to you at this stage.

The following are suggested solutions for the previous McDuck's Offer app research questions. Your answers may vary, so review each answer to see where your code differs from mine:

>> **"The customer presses a button on the app:"** The HTML tag syntax to create a button that says "McDuck's Check-in" is:

```
<button>McDuck's Check-in</button>
```

TIP

The syntax for an HTML button is available here www.w3schools.com/tags/tag_button.asp.

>> **"After the button is pressed, find the customer's current location:"** The HTML syntax for your button code is:

```
<button onclick="getLocation()">McDuck's Check-in</button>
```

TIP

The syntax for calling a JavaScript function by pressing a button is available here www.w3schools.com/jsref/event_onclick.asp.

>> **"Find the fixed location of a McDuck's store:"** I picked a McDonald's store in New York City near Madison Square Park whose latitude is 40.7410344 and longitude is –73.9880763. The latitude and longitude for your restaurant, of course, will likely differ.

» **"Calculate the distance between the customer's current location and the McDuck's restaurant, and name this distance Customer Distance:"** The following is the actual code for the Haversine formula, used to calculate the distance between two location coordinates, found on Stackoverflow at stackoverflow.com/questions/27928/how-do-i-calculate-distance-between-two-latitude-longitude-points, I modified this code slightly so that it returned miles instead of kilometers:

```
function getDistanceFromLatLonInKm(lat1,lon1,lat2,lon2) {
  var R = 6371; // Radius of the earth in km
  var dLat = deg2rad(lat2-lat1);  // deg2rad below
  var dLon = deg2rad(lon2-lon1);
  var a =
    Math.sin(dLat/2) * Math.sin(dLat/2) +
    Math.cos(deg2rad(lat1)) * Math.cos(deg2rad(lat2)) *
    Math.sin(dLon/2) * Math.sin(dLon/2)
    ;
  var c = 2 * Math.atan2(Math.sqrt(a), Math.sqrt(1-a));
  var d = R * c * 0.621371; // Distance in miles
  return d;
}


function deg2rad(deg) {
  return deg * (Math.PI/180);
}
```

TIP An explanation of how this formula works is outside the scope of this book, but make sure you understand the formula's inputs (latitude and longitude) and the output (distance between two points in miles).

» **"Convert five to ten minutes of customer travel into a distance called _Threshold Distance:_"** In New York City, people usually walk, so traveling for five to ten minutes would take you 0.5 miles, which is my Threshold Distance.

» **"If the Customer Distance is less than the Threshold Distance, then display an offer to the customer:"** The syntax for the if-else statement with the two text alert( ) methods is:

```
If (distance < 0.5) {
    alert("You get a free burger");
}
else {
    alert("Thanks for checking in!");
}
```

TIP The syntax for a JavaScript if-else statement is available at www.w3schools.com/js/js_if_else.asp.

Chapter 12

Coding and Debugging Your First Web Application

Talk is cheap. Show me the code.

—LINUS TORVALDS

I t may not feel like it, but you've already done the majority of work toward creating your first web application. You painfully broke down your app into steps, and researched each step to determine functionality and design. As Linus Torvalds, creator of the Linux operator system, said, "Talk is cheap." So let's start actually coding.

Getting Ready to Code

Before you start coding, do a few housekeeping items. First, ensure that you are doing all of the following:

>> **Using the Chome browser:** Download and install the latest version of Chome, as it offers the most support for the latest HTML standards, and is available for download at www.google.com/chrome/browser.

>> **Working on a desktop or laptop computer:** Although it is possible to code on a mobile device, it can be more difficult and all layouts may not appear properly.

>> **Remembering to indent your code to make it easier to read:** One main source of mistakes is forgetting to close a tag or curly brace, and indenting your code will make spotting these errors easier.

>> **Remembering to enable location services on your browser and computer:** To enable location services within Chrome, click on the settings icon (3 horizontal lines on the top right of the browser), and click on Settings. Then click on the Settings tab, and at the bottom of the screen click on "Show Advanced settings..." Under the Privacy menu heading, click on "Content settings..." and scroll down to Location and make sure that "Ask when a site tries to track your physical location" is selected. You can read more here: support.google.com/chrome/answer/142065.

To enable location services on a PC no additional setting is necessary, but on a Mac using OS X Mountain Lion or later, from the Apple menu choose System Preferences, then click on the Security & Privacy icon, and click the Privacy tab. Click the padlock icon on the lower left, and select Location Services, and check Enable Location Services. You can read more here: support.apple.com/en-us/ht5403.

Finally, you need to set up your development environment. To emulate a development environment without instructional content use Codepen.io. Codepen.io offers a free stand-alone development environment, and makes it easy to share your code. Open this URL in in your browser: codepen.io/nabraham/pen/ExnsA.

Coding Your First Web Application

With the Codepen.io URL loaded, let us review the development environment, the pre-written code, and the coding steps for you to follow.

Development environment

The Codepen.io development environment, as shown in Figure 12-1, has three coding panels, one each for HTML, CSS, and JavaScript. There is also a preview pane to see the live results of your code. Using the button at the bottom of the screen, you can hide any coding panel you aren't using, and the layout of the coding panels can be changed.

Signing up for a Codepen.io account is completely optional, and allows you to *fork* or save the code you have written, and share it with others.

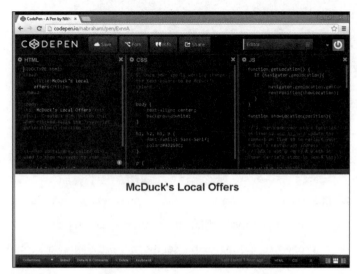

FIGURE 12-1:
The Codepen.io development environment.

Pre-written code

The Codepen.io development environment includes some pre-written HTML, CSS, and JavaScript code for the McDuck's app. The pre-written code includes code you have seen in previous chapters, and new code that is explained below:

>> **HTML:** The HTML code for the McDuck's app is below, and includes

- Two sections: an opening and closing ‹head› tag, and an opening and closing ‹body› tag.

- Inside the ‹body› tags are ‹h1› tags to create a heading and ‹div› tags.

- Additional ‹div› tags to display messages created in the JavaScript file. The ‹div› tag is a container that can hold content of any type. The first ‹div› tag is used to display your current longitude and latitude. The second ‹div› tag can be used to display additional content to the user.

- Instructions to insert the HTML button and onclick attribute code, which you researched in previous chapters.

Here's the HTML code:

```
<!DOCTYPE html>
<html>
<head>
  <title>McDuck's App</title>
</head>
<body>
  <h1> McDuck's Local Offers</h1>
```

```
<!--1. Create a HTML button that when clicked calls the JavaScript getLocation()
    function -->

<!--Two containers, called divs, used to show messages to user -->

  <div id="geodisplay"/>
  <div id="effect"/>

</body>
</html>
```

>> **CSS:** The CSS code for the McDuck's app is below, and includes:

- Selectors for the body, heading, and paragraph tags.

- Properties and values that set the text alignment, background color, font family, font color, and font size.

Once your app is functioning, style the app by adding a McDuck's color scheme and background image logo.

Here's the CSS:

```
body {
    text-align: center;
    background: white;
}


h1, h2, h3, p {
    font-family: Sans-Serif;
    color: black;
}


p {
    font-size: 1em;
}
```

>> **JavaScript:** The JavaScript code for the McDuck's app is below. This pre-written code is a little complex, because it calculates the current location of the user using the HTML Geolocation API. In this section I review the code at a high level so you can understand how it works and where it came from.

The Geolocation API is the product of billions of dollars of research and is available to you for free. The most recent browsers support geolocation, though some older browsers do not. At a basic level, code is written to ask whether the browser supports the Geolocation API, and, if yes, to return the current location of the user. When called, the Geolocation API balances a number of data inputs to determine the user's current location. These data inputs include GPS, wireless network connection strength, cell tower and signal strength, and IP address.

With this in mind, let's look at the JavaScript code. The JavaScript code includes two functions, as follows:

- *The getLocation( ) function:* This function determines whether the browser supports geolocation. It does this by using an if statement and navigator.geolocation, which is recognized by the browser as part of the Geolocation API and which returns a true value if geolocation is supported.

Here is the getLocation( ) function:

```
function getLocation() {
    if (navigator.geolocation){
        navigator.geolocation.getCurrentPosition(showLocation);
    }
}
```

- *The showLocation( ) function:* When the browser supports geolocation, the next step is to call the showlocation function, which calculates and displays the user's location.

And here is the showLocation( ) function:

```
function showLocation(position){
// 2. Hardcode your store location on line 12 and 13, and update the comment to
    reflect your McDuck's restaurant address
//  Nik's apt @ Perry & W 4th St (change to your restaurant location)

var mcduckslat=40.735383;
var mcduckslon=-74.002994;

// current location
var currentpositionlat=position.coords.latitude;
var currentpositionlon=position.coords.longitude;

// calculate the distance between current location and McDuck's location
var distance=getDistanceFromLatLonInMiles(mcduckslat, mcduckslon,currentpositionlat,
    currentpositionlon);

// Displays the location using .innerHTML property and the lat & long coordinates
    for your current location
document.getElementById("geodisplay").innerHTML="Latitude: " + currentpositionlat +
    "<br>Longitude: " + currentpositionlon;
}

// haversine distance formula
The rest omitted for brevity because it's shown in a previous chapter
```

The showLocation( ) function performs the following tasks:

- Assigns the McDuck longitude and latitude to mduckslat and mcduckslon (Lines 12 and 13 of the code).

- Assigns the longitude and latitude of the customer's current location to currentpositionlat and currentpositionlon (Lines 16 and 17 of the code).

- Calculates the distance in miles between those two points and assigns that distance to a variable called distance (Line 20 of the code). The Haversine formula calculates the distance between two points on a sphere, in this case the earth, and the code is shown online but omitted here for brevity.

- After the button is clicked, the getElementByID and .innerHTML methods display the customer's current longitude and latitude in an HTML tag named "geodisplay" using the id attribute.

REMEMBER

JavaScript functions are case-sensitive, so getLocation( ) differs from getlocation( ). The letter L is uppercase in the first function, and lowercase in the second function. Similarly, showLocation( ) differs from showlocation( ) for the same reason.

Coding steps for you to follow

With some of the code already written, and with research in the previous chapter, follow these steps to insert the code:

1. Insert the HTML button code below with onclick attribute calling the getLocation( ) function after line 8 in the HTML file.

```
<button onclick="getLocation()">McDuck's Check-in</button>
```

After you insert this code, press the button. If your location settings are enabled and you inserted the code properly, you will see a dialog box asking for your permission to share your computer's location. As shown in Figure 12-2, look at the top of your browser window and click Allow.

2. Update lines 12 and 13 in the JavaScript file with the latitude and longitude of the restaurant near you serving as the McDuck's store.

After you have updated the location, make sure to change the comment in line 10 to reflect the address of your restaurant (instead of my apartment).

FIGURE 12-2:
The browser
asks for your
permission
before sharing
your location.

3. **Add an alert that displays the distance between your location and the restaurant.**

The `distance` variable stores the miles from your current location to the restaurant. Make a rough estimate — or use a map for greater precision — of your current distance from the restaurant you picked. Then using an alert, show the distance by inserting this code below in line 23.

```
alert(distance);
```

If the distance in the alert is larger or smaller than you expected, you likely entered in incorrect values for the latitude or longitude. If the distance matches your estimate, insert two slashes ("//") before the alert and comment it out.

4. **Write an `if-else` statement on line 26 to show an alert if you are within your threshold distance to the restaurant.**

My code, based on a half-mile threshold distance, is displayed below — yours may vary depending on your alert text and threshold distance. (See Figure 12-3.)

```
if (distance < 0.5) {
    alert("You get a free burger");
}
else {
    alert("Thanks for checking in!");
}
```

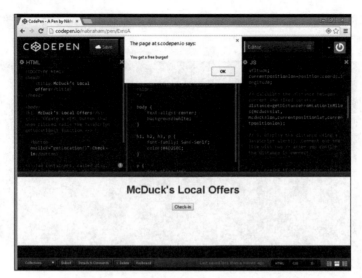

FIGURE 12-3:
The McDuck's
app displaying
an offer to
come to the
store.

TIP

When your app logic is working, you can change alert("You get a free burger"); to an actual picture of a coupon or burger. To do so, replace the entire line the alert is on with the following code:

```
document.getElementById("effect").innerHTML="<img src='http://www.image.com/
    image.jpg'>";
```

Replace the URL after src and within the single quotes to your own image URL. Be sure to keep the double quotation marks after the first equals sign and before the semi-colon, and the single quotation marks after the second equals sign and before the right angle bracket.

5. **(Optional) When the app is working, change the text colors and insert background images to make the app look more professional.**

Use hex-values or color names, as discussed in Chapter 6, to change the text and background colors. Additionally, you can insert a background image, as you did in the Codecademy About You exercise, using the following code (see Figure 12-4):

```
background-image: url("http://www.image.com/image.jpg");
```

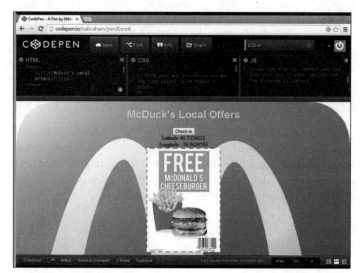

FIGURE 12-4:
The completed McDuck's app with styled content displaying an image to the user.

Debugging Your App

When coding your app, you will almost inevitably write code that does not behave as you intended. HTML and CSS are relatively forgiving, with the browser even going so far as to insert tags so the page renders properly. However, JavaScript isn't so forgiving, and the smallest error, such as a missing quotation mark, can cause the page to not render properly.

Errors in web applications can consist of syntax errors, logic errors, and display errors. Given that we worked through the logic together, the most likely culprit causing errors in your code will be syntax related. Here are some common errors to check when debugging your code:

>> **Opening and closing tags:** In HTML, every opening tag has a closing tag, and you always close the most recently opened tag first.

>> **Right and left angle brackets:** In HTML, every left angle bracket ‹ has a right angle bracket ›.

>> **Right and left curly brackets:** In CSS and JavaScript, every left curly bracket must have a right curly bracket. It can be easy to accidentally delete it or forget to include it.

>> **Indentation:** Indent your code and use plenty of tabs and returns to make your code as readable as possible. Proper indentation will make it easier for you to identify missing tags, angle brackets, and curly brackets.

» **Misspelled statements:** Tags in any language can be misspelled, or spelled correctly but not part of the specification. For example, in HTML, `<img scr="image.jpg">` is incorrect because `scr` should really be `src` for the image to render properly. Similarly, in CSS `font-color` looks like it is spelled correctly but no such property exists. The correct property to set font color is just `color`.

Keep these errors in mind when debugging — they may not solve all your problems, but they should solve many of them. If you have tried the steps above and still cannot debug your code, tweet me at `@nikhilgabraham` and include the `#codingFD` hashtag and your Codepen.io URL in your tweet.

4

Developing Your Coding Skills Further

IN THIS CHAPTER

**Understanding Ruby principles
and style**

Assigning variables and using `if`
statements

**Manipulating strings for consistency
and formatting**

Chapter 13

Getting Familiar with Ruby

*I hope Ruby helps every programmer be productive, enjoy programming, and
be happy. That is the primary purpose of Ruby language.*

— YUKIHIRO MATSUMOTO, CREATOR OF RUBY

Ruby is a server-side language created by Yukihiro "Matz" Matsumoto, a developer who was looking for an easy-to-use scripting language. Matsumoto had experience programming in other languages like Perl and Python, and, unsatisfied with both, created Ruby. When designing Ruby, Matsumoto's explicit goal was to "make programmers happy", and he created the language so programmers could easily learn it and use it. It worked. Today Ruby, and particularly Ruby working with a Ruby framework called Rails, is the most popular way for startups and companies to quickly create prototypes and launch websites on the Internet.

In this chapter, you learn Ruby basics, including its design philosophy; how to write Ruby code to perform basic tasks; and steps to create your first Ruby program.

What Does Ruby Do?

Ruby is a general purpose programming language typically used for web development. Until now, the HTML, CSS, and JavaScript you have learned in the previous chapters has not allowed for storing data after the user has navigated away from the page or closed the browser. Ruby makes it easy to store this data, and create, update, store, and retrieve it in a database. For example, imagine I wanted to create a social networking website like Twitter. The content I write in a tweet is stored in a central database. I can exit my browser, and turn off my computer, but if I come back to the website later my tweets are still accessible to me. Additionally, if others search for me or keywords in the tweets I have written, this same central database is queried, and any matches are displayed. Ruby developers frequently perform tasks like storing information in a database, and a Ruby framework called Rails speeds up development by including pre-built code, templates, and easy ways to perform these tasks. For these reasons, websites frequently use Ruby and Rails together.

A website using the Rails framework is referred to as being built with Rails or "Ruby on Rails."

Twitter's website was one of the most trafficked websites to use Ruby on Rails, and until 2010 used Ruby code for its search and messaging products. Other websites currently using Ruby on Rails include:

» E-commerce websites such as those on the www.shopify.com platform, including The Chivery and Black Milk Clothing.

» Music websites such as www.soundcloud.com.

» Social networking sites such as www.yammer.com.

» News websites such as www.bloomberg.com.

As shown above, Ruby and Rails can create a variety of websites. While Rails emphasizes productivity, allowing developers to quickly write code and test prototypes, some developers criticize Ruby and Rails for not being scalable, and use as evidence Twitter rewriting their code to stop using Rails for many core features. While I cannot resolve the productivity-scalability debate for you here, I can say that Rails can adequately handle millions of visitors per month, and no matter the language used, significant work must be done to scale a website to properly handle tens or hundreds of millions of visitors a month.

Confirm the programming language used by these or any major website with BuiltWith available at www.builtwith.com. After entering the website address in the search bar, look under the Frameworks section for Ruby on Rails.

Defining Ruby Structure

Ruby has its own set of design principles that guide how the rest of the language is structured. All the languages you have learned so far have their own conventions, like the curly braces in JavaScript or opening and closing tags in HTML, and Ruby is no different with conventions of its own. The design principles in Ruby explain how Ruby tries to be different from the programming languages that came before it. With these design principles in mind you will then see what Ruby code looks like, understand Ruby's style, and learn the special keywords and syntax that allow the computer to recognize what you are trying to do. Unlike HTML and CSS, and similar to JavaScript, Ruby can be particular about syntax and misspelling a keyword or forgetting a necessary character will result in the program not running.

Understanding the principles of Ruby

Ruby has a few design principles to make programming in the language less stressful and more fun for programmers of other programming languages. These design principles are:

» **Principle of conciseness:** In general, short and concise code is needed to create programs. The initial set of steps to run a program written in English is often referred to as pseudo-code. Ruby is designed so as little additional effort is needed to translate pseudo-code into actual code. Even existing Ruby commands can be made more concise. For example, Ruby's `if` statement can be written in three lines or just one.

» **Principle of consistency:** A small set of rules governs the entire language. Sometimes this principle in referred to as the principle of least astonishment or principle of least surprise. In general, if you are familiar with another programming language, the way Ruby behaves should feel intuitive for you. For example, in JavaScript when working with string methods, you can chain them together like so:

```
"alphabet".toUpperCase().concat("Soup")
```

This JavaScript statement returns "ALPHABETSoup" by first making the string "alphabet" uppercase using the `.toUpperCase()` method, and then concatenating "soup" to "ALPHABET". Similarly, the Ruby statement below chains together methods just as you would expect, also returning "ALPHABETSoup".

```
"alphabet".upcase.concat("Soup")
```

» **Principle of flexibility:** There are multiple ways to accomplish the same thing, and even built-in commands can be changed. For example, when writing an `if-else` statement you can use the words `if` and `else`, but you can also accomplish the task with a single "?". The following code both perform the same task.

Version 1:

```ruby
if 3>4
    puts "the condition is true"
else
    puts "the condition is false"
end
```

Version 2:

```ruby
puts 3>4 ? "the condition is false" : "the condition is true"
```

Styling and spacing

Ruby generally uses less punctuation than other programming languages you may have previously tried. Some sample code is included below.

```ruby
print "What's your first name?"
first_name = gets.chomp
first_name.upcase!

if first_name=="NIK"
    print "You may enter!"
else
    print "Nothing to see here."
end
```

If you ran this code it would do the following:

›› Print a line asking for your first name.

›› Take user input (gets.chomp) and save it to the first_name variable.

›› Test the user input. If it equals "NIK" then print "You may enter!" otherwise print "Nothing to see here."

Each of these statement types is covered in more detail later in this chapter. For now, as you look at the code, notice some of its styling characteristics

›› Less punctuation: unlike JavaScript there are no curly braces, and unlike HTML there are no angle brackets.

›› Spaces, tabs, and indentation are ignored: unless within a text string whitespace characters do not matter.

» Newlines indicate the end of statements: although you can use semi-colons to put more than one statement on a line, the preferred and more common method is to put each statement on its own line.

» Dot-notation is frequently used: the period (as in .chomp or .upcase) signals the use of a method, which is common in Ruby. A method is a set of instructions that carry out a particular task. In this code example, .chomp removes carriage returns from the user input, and .upcase transforms the user input into all upper case.

» Exclamation points signal danger: methods applied to variables, like first_name.upcase, by default do not change the variable's value and only transform a copy of the variable's value. Exclamation points signal a permanent change, so first_name.upcase! permanently changes the value of the variable first_name.

Coding Common Ruby Tasks and Commands

Ruby can perform many tasks from simple text manipulation to complex login and password user authentication. The following basic tasks, while explained within a Ruby context, are core programming concepts applicable to any programming language. If you have read about another programming language in this book, the following will look familiar. These tasks all take place in the Ruby shell, which looks like a command line interface. Ruby can also generate HTML to create interactive web pages, but that is slightly more complex and not covered here.

Instructions on how to do these basic tasks are below, but you can also practice these skills right away by jumping ahead to the "Building a Simple Form-Text Formatter Using Ruby" section, later in this chapter.

TIP

Programming languages can do the same set of tasks, and understanding the set of tasks in one language makes it easier to understand the next language.

Defining data types and variables

Variables, like in algebra, are keywords used to store data values for later use. Though the data stored in a variable may change, the variable name will always be the same. Think of a variable like a gym locker — what you store in the locker changes, but the locker number always stays the same.

Variables in Ruby are named using alphanumeric characters and the underscore (_) character, and cannot begin with a number or capital letter. Table 13-1 lists some of the data types that Ruby can store.

TABLE 13-1 **Data Stored by a Variable**

Data Type	Description	Example
Numbers	Positive or negative numbers with or without decimals	156–101.96
Strings	Printable characters	Holly NovakSeñor
Boolean	Value can either be true or false	truefalse

To initially set or change a variable's value, write the variable name and use one equals sign, as shown in the following example:

```
myName = "Nik"
pizzaCost = 10
totalCost = pizzaCost * 2
```

TIP

Unlike JavaScript, Ruby does not require you to use the var keyword to declare a variable, or to set its value the first time.

Variable names are case sensitive, so when referring to a variable in your program remember that MyName is a different variable from myname. In general, give your variable a name that describes the data being stored.

Computing simple and advanced math

After you create variables, you may want to do some math on the numerical values stored in those variables. Simple math like addition, subtraction, multiplication, and division is done using operators you already know. One difference is exponentiation (such as, for example, 2 to the power of 3) is done using two asterisks. Examples are shown below, and in Table 13-2.

```
sum1 = 1+1   (equals 2)
sum1 = 5-1   (equals 4)
sum1 = 3*4   (equals 12)
sum1 = 9/3   (equals 3)
sum1 = 2**3  (equals 8)
```

Advanced math like absolute value, rounding to the nearest decimal, rounding up, or rounding down can be performed using number methods, which are shortcuts to make performing certain tasks easier. The general syntax is to follow the variable name or value with a period, and the name of the method as follows for values and variables:

```
value.method
variable.method
```

The values and variables that methods act upon are called objects. If you compared Ruby to the English language, think of objects like nouns and methods like verbs.

TABLE 13-2   **Common Ruby Number Methods**

Method Name	Description	Example	Result
.abs	Returns the absolute value of a number	-99.abs	99
.round(ndigits)	Rounds a number to n digits	3.1415.round(2)	3.14
.floor	Rounds down to the nearest integer	4.7.floor	4
.ceil	Rounds up to the nearest integer	7.3.ceil	8

Using strings and special characters

Along with numbers, variables in Ruby can also store strings. To assign a value to a string use single or double quotation marks.

```
firstname = "Jack"
lastname = 'Dorsey'
```

To display these variable values, you can `puts` or `print` the variable value to the screen. The difference between the two is `puts` adds a newline (ie., carriage return) after displaying the value, while `print` does not.

Variables can also store numbers as strings instead of numbers. Even though the string looks like a number, Ruby will not be able to perform any operations on it. For example, Ruby cannot evaluate this code as is: `amountdue = "18" + 24`.

One issue arises with strings and variables — what if your string itself includes a single or double quote? For example, if I want to store a string with the value 'I'm on my way home' or "Carrie said she was leaving for "just a minute"". As is, the double or single quotes within the string would cause problems with variable assignment. The solution is to use special characters called escape sequences to indicate when you want to use characters like quotation marks, which normally signal the beginning or end of a string, or other non-printable characters like tabs. Table 13-3 shows some examples of escape sequences.

TABLE 13-3   **Common Ruby Escape Sequences**

Special Character	Description	Example	Result
\' or \"	Quotation marks	`print "You had me at \"Hello\""`	`You had me at "Hello"`
\t	Tab	`print "Item\tUnits \tPrice"`	`Item Units Price`

\n	Newline	`print "Anheuser?\nBusch?\n Bueller? Bueller?"`	`Anheuser?`
			 `Busch?`
			 `Bueller? Bueller?`

Escape sequences are interpreted only for strings with double quotation marks. For a full list of escape sequences, see `http://en.wikibooks.org/wiki/ Ruby_Programming/Strings`.

Deciding with conditionals: if, elsif, else

With data stored in a variable, one common task is to compare the variable's value to a fixed value or another variable's value, and then make a decision based on the comparison. If you previously read the JavaScript chapter, you may recall much of the same discussion, and the concept is exactly the same. The general syntax for an `if-elsif-else` statement is as follows:

```
if conditional1
    statement1 to execute if conditional1 is true
elsif conditional2
    statement2 to execute if conditional2 is true
else
    statement3 to run if all previous conditionals are false
end
```

Notice there is only one 'e' in `elsif` statement.

The `if` is followed by a conditional, which evaluates to `true` or `false`. If the condition is `true`, then the statement is executed. This is the minimum necessary syntax needed for an `if-statement`, and the `elseif` and `else` are optional. If present, the elsif tests for an additional condition when the first conditional is false. You can test for as many conditions as you like using elsif. Specifying every condition to test for can become tedious, so it is useful to have a "catch-all." If present, the else serves this function, and executes when all previous conditionals are false.

You cannot have an elsif or an else by itself, without a preceding if statement. You can include many elsif statements, but one and only one else statement.

The conditional in an if statement compares values using comparison operators, and common comparison operators are described in Table 13-4.

TABLE 13-4 **Common Ruby Comparison Operators**

Type	Operator	Description	Example
Less than	<	Evaluates whether one value is less than another value	x < 55
Greater than	>	Evaluates whether one value is greater than another value	x > 55
Equality	==	Evaluates whether two values are equal	x == 55
Less than or equal to	<=	Evaluates whether one value is less than or equal to another value	x <= 55
Greater than or equal to	>=	Evaluates whether one value is greater than or equal to another value	x >= 55
Inequality	!=	Evaluates whether two values are not equal	x != 55

Here is an example if statement.

```
carSpeed=40
if carSpeed > 55
    print "You are over the speed limit!"
elsif carSpeed == 55
    print "You are at the speed limit!"
else
    print "You are under the speed limit!"
end
```

As the diagram in Figure 13-1 shows, there are two conditions, each signaled by the diamond, which are evaluated in sequence. In this example, carSpeed is equal to 40, so the first condition (carSpeed > 55) is false, and then the second conditional (carSpeed==55) is also false. With both conditionals false, the else executes and prints to the screen "You are under the speed limit!"

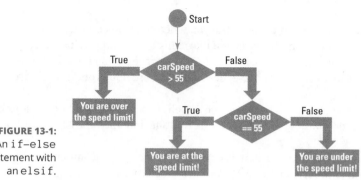

FIGURE 13-1:
An if–else
statement with
an elsif.

Input and output

As you have seen in this chapter, Ruby allows you to collect input from and display output to the user. To collect user input use the `gets` method, which stores the user input as a string. In the following example, the user enters his first name which is stored in a variable called `full_name`:

```
print "What's your full name?"
full_name = gets
```

TECHNICAL
STUFF

`gets` might sound like an odd keyword to collect user input. Ruby is influenced by the C programming language, which also has a `gets` function to collect user input.

Imagine the user entered his name, "Satya Nadella." As the code is currently written, if you display the value of the variable `full_name` you would see this:

```
Satya Nadella\n
```

The \n escape sequence appears after the name because after asking for input the user pressed the "Enter" key, which Ruby stores as \n. To remove the \n add the chomp method to the string, and it will remove the \n and \r escape sequences.

```
print "What's your full name?"
full_name = gets.chomp
```

Now when you display the `full_name` variable you would only see "Satya Nadella".

To display output to the user you can either use `print` or `puts`, short for "put string." The difference between the two is that `puts` adds a newline after executing, while print does not. The following code shows the difference when `print` and `puts` is executed.

Print code:

```
print "The mission has "
print "great tacos"
```

Result:

```
The mission has great tacos
```

Puts code:

```
puts "The mission has "
puts "great tacos"
```

Result:

```
The mission has
great tacos
```

Shaping Your Strings

Manipulating strings is one of the most common tasks for a programmer. Sample tasks in this category include:

>> Standardizing strings to have consistent upper- and lowercase.

>> Removing white space from user input.

>> Inserting variables values in strings displayed to the user.

Ruby shines when it comes to dealing with strings, and includes many built-in methods that make processing strings easier in Ruby than in other languages.

String methods: upcase, downcase, strip

Standardizing user input to have proper case and remove extra white space characters is often necessary to easily search the data later. For example, imagine you are designing a website for the New York Department of Motor Vehicles, and one page is for driver license application and renewals. Both the application and renewal forms ask for current address, which includes a field for two letter state abbreviation. After reviewing completed paper forms, and previous electronic data you see that drivers enter the state in several ways including "NY", "ny", "Ny", " ny ", "nY", and other similar variants. If "NY" was the desired result you could use upcase and strip to make this input consistent. Table 13-5 further describes these string methods.

TABLE 13-5 **Select Ruby String Methods**

Method Name	Description	Example	Result
upcase	Returns all uppercase characters	"nY".upcase	"NY"
downcase	Returns all lowercase characters	"Hi".downcase	"hi"
capitalize	Capitalizes first letter, lowercases remaining letters	"wake UP".capitalize	"Wake up"
strip	Removes leading and trailing whitespaces	" Ny ".strip	"Ny"

Inserting variables in strings with

To insert variable values into strings shown to the user, you can use the hashtag sequence #{...}. The code between the open and closing curly braces is evaluated and inserted into the string. Like with escape sequences, the variable value is inserted only into strings created with double quotation marks. See the example code and result below.

Code:

```
yearofbirth = 1990
pplinroom = 20
puts "Your year of birth is #{yearofbirth}. Is this correct?"
puts 'Your year of birth is #{yearofbirth}. Is this correct?'
puts "There are #{pplinroom / 2} women in the room with the same birth year."
```

Result:

```
Your year of birth is 1990. Is this correct?
Your year of birth is #{yearofbirth}. Is this correct?
There are 10 women in the room with the same birth year.
```

The first string used double quotes and the variable was inserted into the string and displayed to the user. The second string used single quotes so the code inside the curly braces was not evaluated, the variable value was not inserted, and instead #{yearofbirth} was displayed. The third string shows that any code can be evaluated and inserted into the string.

TECHNICAL STUFF

This method of inserting variable values into strings is called string interpolation.

Building a Simple Form-Text Formatter Using Ruby

Practice your Ruby online using the Codecademy website. Codecademy is a free website created in 2011 to allow anyone to learn how to code right in the browser, without installing or downloading any software. Practice all of the tags (and a few more) that you learned in this chapter by following these steps:

1. **Open your browser, go to** www.dummies.com/go/codingfd, **and click on the link to Codecademy.**

2. **Sign in to your Codecademy account.**

   Signing up is discussed in Chapter 3. Creating an account allows you to save your progress as you work, but it's optional.

3. **Navigate to and click on Introduction to Ruby to practice some basic Ruby commands.**

4. **Background information is presented in the upper left portion of the site, and instructions are presented in the lower left portion of the site.**

5. **Complete the instructions in the main coding window.**

6. **After you have finished completing the instructions, click the Save and Submit Code button.**

   If you have followed the instructions correctly, a green checkmark appears, and you proceed to the next exercise. If an error exists in your code a warning appears with a suggested fix. If you run into a problem, or have a bug you cannot fix, click on the hint, use the Q&A Forums, or tweet me at @nikhilgabraham and include hashtag #codingFD.

Chapter 14

Wrapping Your Head around Python

I chose Python as a working title for the project, being in a slightly irreverent mood (and a big fan of Monty Python's Flying Circus).

— GUIDO VAN ROSSUM, CREATOR OF PYTHON

Python is a server-side language created by Guido van Rossum, a developer who was bored during the winter of 1989 and looking for a project to do. At the time, Van Rossum had already helped create one language, called ABC, and the experience had given him many ideas that he thought would appeal to programmers. He executed upon these ideas when he created Python. Although ABC never achieved popularity with programmers, Python was a runaway success. Python is one of the world's most popular programming languages, used by beginners just starting out and professionals building heavy-duty applications.

In this chapter, you learn Python basics, including the design philosophy behind Python, how to write Python code to perform basic tasks, and steps to create your first Python program.

What Does Python Do?

Python is a general purpose programming language typically used for web development. This may sound similar to the description used for Ruby in the previous chapter, and really both languages are more similar than they are different. Python, like Ruby, allows for storing data after the user has navigated away from the page or closed the browser, unlike HTML, CSS, and JavaScript. Using Python commands you can create, update, store, and retrieve this data in a database. For example, imagine I wanted to create a local search and ratings site like Yelp.com. The reviews users write are stored in a central database. Any review author can exit the browser, turn off the computer, and come back to the website later to find their reviews. Additionally, when others search for venues, this same central database is queried, and the same review is displayed. Storing data in a database is a common task for Python developers, and existing Python libraries include pre-built code to easily create and query databases.

TECHNICAL STUFF

SQLite is one free lightweight database commonly used by Python programmers to store data.

Many highly trafficked websites, such as YouTube, are created using Python. Other websites currently using Python include:

>> Quora for its community question and answer site.

>> Spotify for internal data analysis.

>> Dropbox for its desktop client software.

>> Reddit for generating crowd-sourced news.

>> Industrial Light & Magic and Disney Animation for creating film special effects.

From websites to software to special effects, Python is an extremely versatile language, powerful enough to support a range of applications. In addition, to help spread Python code, Python programmers create libraries, which are stand-alone pre-written code that do certain tasks, and make them publicly available for others to use and improve. For example, a library called Scrapy performs web scaping, while another library called SciPy performs math functions used by scientists and mathematicians. The Python community maintains thousands of libraries like these, and most are free and open-source software.

TIP

You can generally confirm the front-end programming language used by any major website with BuiltWith available at www.builtwith.com. After entering the website address in the search bar, look under the Frameworks section for Python. Note that websites may use Python for backend services not visible to BuiltWith.

Defining Python Structure

Python has its own set of design principles that guide how the rest of the language is structured. To implement these principles, every language has its own conventions, like curly braces in JavaScript or opening and closing tags in HTML. Python is no different, and we will cover both design principles and conventions so you can understand what Python code looks like, understand Python's style, and learn the special keywords and syntax that allow the computer to recognize what you are trying to do. Python, like Ruby and JavaScript, can be very particular about syntax, and misspelling a keyword or forgetting a necessary character will result in the program not running.

Understanding the Zen of Python

There are nineteen design principles that describe how the Python language is organized. Some of the most important principles include

>> **Readability counts:** This is possibly Python's most important design principle. Python code looks almost like English, and even enforces certain formatting, such as indenting, to make the code easier to read. Highly readable code means that six months from now when you revisit your code to fix a bug or add a feature, you will be able to jump in without trying too hard to remember what you did. Readable code also means others can use your code or help debug your code with ease.

TECHNICAL
STUFF

Reddit.com is a top-10-most-visited website in the US, and a top-50-most-visited website in the world. Its co-founder, Steve Huffman, initially coded the website in Lisp and switched to Python because Python is "extremely readable, and extremely writeable."

>> **There should be one — and preferably *only* one — obvious way to do it:** This principle is directly opposite to Perl's motto, "There's more than one way to do it." In Python, two different programmers may approach the same problem and write two different programs, but the ideal is that the code will be similar and easy to read, adopt, and understand. Although Python does allow multiple ways to do a task — as, for example, when combining two strings — if an obvious and common option exists, it should be used.

>> **If the implementation is hard to explain, it's a bad idea:** Historically, programmers were known to write esoteric code to increase performance. However, Python was designed not to be the fastest language, and this principle reminds programmers that easy-to-understand implementations are preferable over faster but harder-to-explain ones.

TIP

Access the full list by design principles, which is in the form of a poem, by typing `import this;` into any Python interpreter, or by visiting https://www.python.org/dev/peps/pep-0020. These principles, written by Tim Peters, a Python community member, were meant to describe the intentions of Python's creator, Van Rossum, who is also referred to as the Benevolent Dictator for Life (BDFL).

Styling and spacing

Python generally uses less punctuation than other programming languages you may have previously tried. Some sample code is included here:

```
first_name=raw_input("What's your first name?")
first_name=first_name.upper()

if first_name=="NIK":
    print "You may enter!"
else:
    print "Nothing to see here."
```

TECHNICAL STUFF

The examples in this book are written for Python 2.7. There are two popular version of Python currently in use — Python 2.7 and Python 3. Python 3 is the latest version of the language but it is not backwards-compatible, so code written using Python 2.7 syntax does not work when using a Python 3 interpreter. Initially, Python 2.7 had more external libraries and support than Python 3, but this is changing. For more about the differences between versions see https://wiki.python.org/moin/Python2orPython3.

If you ran this code it would do the following:

>> Print a line asking for your first name.

>> Take user input (raw_input(What's your first name?)) and save it to the first_name variable.

>> Transform any inputted text into uppercase.

>> Test the user input. If it equals "NIK," then it will print "You may enter!" Otherwise it will print "Nothing to see here."

Each of these statement types is covered in more detail later in this chapter. For now, as you look at the code, notice some of its styling characteristics:

>> **Less punctuation:** Unlike JavaScript, Python has no curly braces, and unlike HTML, no angle brackets.

TIP

>> **Whitespace matters:** Statements indented to the same level are grouped together. In the example above, notice how the if and else align, and the print statements underneath each are indented the same amount. You can decide the amount of indentation, and whether to use tabs or spaces as long as you are consistent. Generally, four spaces from the left margin is considered the style norm.

See Python style suggestions on indentation, whitespaces, and commenting by visiting https://www.python.org/dev/peps/pep-0008.

>> **Newlines indicate the end of statements:** Although you can use semi-colons to put more than one statement on a line, the preferred and more common method is to put each statement on its own line.

>> **Colons separate code blocks:** New Python programmers sometimes ask why using colons to indicate code blocks, like the one at the end of the if statement, is necessary when newlines would suffice. Early user testing with and without the colons showed that beginner programmers better understood the code with the colon.

Coding Common Python Tasks and Commands

Python, as with other programming languages like Ruby, can do everything from simple text manipulation to designing complex graphics in games. The following basic tasks are explained within a Python context, but they're foundational in understanding any programming language. Even experienced developers learning a new language, like Apple's recently released Swift programming language, start by learning these foundational tasks. If you have already read the chapter on Ruby, the code to perform these tasks will look similar.

Start learning some basic Python below, or practice these skills right away by jumping ahead to the "Building a Simple Tip Calculator Using Python" section, later in this chapter.

TIP

Millions of people have learned Python before you, so it's easy to find answers to questions that might arise while learning simply by conducting an Internet search. The odds are in your favor that someone has asked your question before.

Defining data types and variables

Variables, like the ones in algebra, are keywords used to store data values for later use. Though the data stored in a variable may change, the variable name will always be the same. Think of a variable as a gym locker — what you store in the locker changes, but the locker number always stays the same.

Variables in Python are named using alphanumeric characters and the underscore (_) character, and they must start with a letter or an underscore. Table 14-1 lists some of the data types that Python can store.

TABLE 14-1 **Data Stored by a Variable**

Data Type	Description	Example
Numbers	Positive or negative numbers with or without decimals	156–101.96
Strings	Printable characters	Holly NovakSeñor
Boolean	Value can either be true or false	truefalse

To initially set or change a variable's value, write the variable name, a single equals sign, and the variable value, as shown in the following example:

```
myName = "Nik"
pizzaCost = 10
totalCost = pizzaCost * 2
```

TIP

Avoid starting your variable names with the number one (1), a lowercase "L" (l), or uppercase i (I). Depending on the font used these characters can all look the same, causing confusion for you or others later!

Variable names are case sensitive, so when referring to a variable in your program remember that MyName is a different variable from myname. In general, give your variable a name that describes the data being stored.

Computing simple and advanced math

After you create variables, you may want to do some math on the numerical values stored in those variables. Simple math like addition, subtraction, multiplication, and division is done using operators you already know. Exponentiation (such as, for example, 2 to the power of 3) is done differently in Python than in JavaScript, and uses two asterisks. Examples are shown here:

```
num1 = 1+1    #equals 2
num2 = 5-1    #equals 4
num3 = 3*4    #equals 12
num4 = 9/3    #equals 3
num5 = 2**3   #equals 8
```

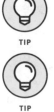

The # symbol indicates a comment in Python.

Don't just read these commands, try them! Go to http://repl.it/languages/Python for a lightweight in-browser Python interpreter that you can use right in your browser without downloading or installing any software.

Advanced math like absolute value, rounding to the nearest decimal, rounding up, or rounding down can be performed using math functions. Python has some functions which are built-in pre-written code that can be referenced to make performing certain tasks easier. The general syntax to use Python math functions is to list the function name, followed by the variable name or value as an argument, as follows:

```
method(value)
method(variable)
```

The math functions for absolute value and rounding follow the syntax above, but some math functions, like rounding up or rounding down are stored in a separate math module. To use these math functions you must:

» Write the statement import math just once in your code before using the math functions in the math module.

» Reference the math module, as follows: math.method(value) or math.method(variable).

See these math functions with examples in Table 14-2.

TABLE 14-2 **Common Python Math Functions**

Function Name	Description	Example	Result
abs(n)	Return the absolute value of a number (n)	abs(-99)	99
round (n, d)	Round a number (n) to a number of decimal points (d)	round (3.1415, 2)	3.14
math.floor(n)	Round down to the nearest integer	math.floor(4.7)	4.0
math.ceil(n)	Round up to the nearest integer	math.ceil(7.3)	8.0

TECHNICAL STUFF

Modules are separate files that contain Python code, and the module must be referenced or imported before any code from the module can be used.

TIP

See all the function in the math module by visiting `https://docs.python.org/2/library/math.html`.

Using strings and special characters

Along with numbers, variables in Python can also store strings. To assign a value to a string you can use single or double quotation marks, as follows:

```
firstname = "Travis"
lastname = 'Kalanick'
```

REMEMBER

Variables can also store numbers as strings instead of numbers. However, even though the string looks like a number, Python will not be able to add, subtract, or divide strings and numbers. For example, consider `amountdue = "18" + 24` — running this code as is would result in an error. Python does multiply strings but in an interesting way — `print 'Ha' * 3` results in `'HaHaHa'`.

Including a single or double quote in your string can be problematic because the quotes inside your string will terminate the string definition prematurely. For example, if I want to store a string with the value 'I'm on my way home' Python will assume the ' after the first letter I is the end of the variable assignment, and the remaining characters will cause an error. The solution is to use special characters called escape sequences to indicate when you want to use characters like quotation marks, which normally signal the beginning or end of a string, or other non-printable characters like tabs. Table 14-3 shows some examples of escape sequences.

TABLE 14-3   **Common Python Escape Sequences**

Special Character	Description	Example	Result
\' or \"	Quotation marks	`print "You had me at \"Hello\""`	You had me at "Hello"
\t	Tab	`print "Item\tUnits \tPrice"`	Item Units Price
\n	Newline	`print "Anheuser?\nBusch? \ nBueller? Bueller?"`	Anheuser? Busch? Bueller? Bueller?

TIP

Escape sequences are interpreted only for strings with double quotation marks. For a full list of escape sequences see the table under Section 2.4 "Literals" at `http://docs.python.org/2/reference/lexical_analysis.html`.

Deciding with conditionals: if, elif, else

With data stored in a variable, one common task is to compare the variable's value to a fixed value or another variable's value, and then make a decision based on the comparison. If you previously read the chapters on JavaScript or Ruby, the discussion and concepts here are very similar. The general syntax for an if-elif-else statement is as follows:

```
if conditional1:
    statement1 to execute if conditional1 is true
elif conditional2:
    statement2 to execute if conditional2 is true
else:
    statement3 to run if all previous conditional are false
```

TIP

Notice there are no curly brackets or semi-colons, but don't forget the colons and to indent your statements!

The initial if statement will evaluate to true or false. When conditional1 is true, then *statement1* is executed. This is the minimum necessary syntax needed for an if-statement, and the elif and else are optional. When present, the elif tests for an additional condition when conditional1 is false. You can test for as many conditions as you like using elif. Specifying every condition to test for can become tedious, so having a "catch-all" is useful. When present, the else serves as the "catch-all," and executes when all previous conditionals are false.

TIP

You cannot have an elif or an else by itself, without a preceding if statement. You can include many elif statements, but one and only one else statement.

The conditional in an if statement compares values using comparison operators, and common comparison operators are described in Table 14-4.

TABLE 14-4   ## Common Python Comparison Operators

Type	Operator	Description	Example
Less than	<	Evaluates whether one value is less than another value	x < 55
Greater than	>	Evaluates whether one value is greater than another value	x > 55
Equality	==	Evaluates whether two values are equal	x == 55
Less than or equal to	<=	Evaluates whether one value is less than or equal to another value	x <= 55
Greater than or equal to	>=	Evaluates whether one value is greater than or equal to another value	x >= 55
Inequality	!=	Evaluates whether two values are not equal	x != 55

Here is an example if statement.

```
carSpeed=55
if carSpeed > 55:
    print "You are over the speed limit!"
elif carSpeed == 55:
    print "You are at the speed limit!"
else:
    print "You are under the speed limit!"
```

As the diagram in Figure 14-1 shows, there are two conditions, each signaled by the diamond, which are evaluated in sequence. In this example, carSpeed is equal to 55, so the first condition (carSpeed > 55) is false, and then the second conditional (carSpeed==55) is true and the statement executes printing "You are at the speed limit!" When a conditional is true, the if statement stops executing, and the else is never reached.

Input and output

Python can collect input from the user, and display output to the user. To collect user input use the raw_input("Prompt") method, which stores the user input as a string. In the example below, the user enters his full name which is stored in a variable called full_name.

```
full_name = raw_input("What's your full name?")
```

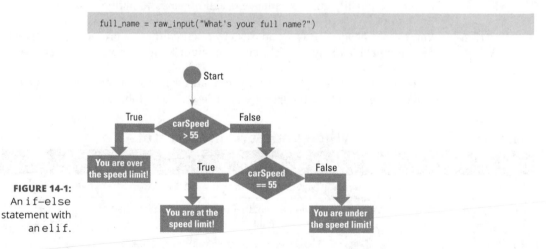

FIGURE 14-1:
An if—else
statement with
an elif.

Imagine the user entered his name, "Jeff Bezos." You can display the value of the variable using print full_name and you would see this:

```
Jeff Bezos
```

TIP

Python, unlike Ruby, does not store the newline \n escape sequence after user input.

At this point, you may feel like printing variables and values in a Python interpreter console window is very different from dynamically creating web pages with variables created in Python. Integrating Python into a web page to respond to user requests and generate HTML pages is typically done with a Python web framework, like Django or Flask, which have pre-written code to make the process easier. These frameworks typically require some installation and set-up work, and generally separate the data being displayed from templates used to display the page to the user.

Shaping Your Strings

Whenever you collect input from users, you need to clean the input to remove errors and inconsistencies. Here are some common data cleaning tasks:

>> Standardizing strings to have consistent upper and lower case

>> Removing white space from user input

>> Inserting a variable's value in strings displayed to the user

Python includes many built-in methods that make processing strings easy.

Dot notation with upper(), lower(), capitalize(), and strip()

Standardizing user input to have proper case and remove extra white space characters is often necessary to easily sort the data later. For example, imagine you are designing a website for the New York Knicks so fans can meet players after the game. The page asks for fans to enter their name, so that team security can later check fan names against this list before entry. Reviewing past fan entries you see that fans enter the same name several ways like "Mark", "mark", "marK", and other similar variants that cause issues when the list is sorted alphabetically. To make the input and these names consistent you could use the string functions described in Table 14-5.

TABLE 14-5
Select Python String Functions

Function Name	Description	Example	Result
`string.upper()`	Returns all uppercase characters	`"nY".upper()`	`"NY"`
`string.lower()`	Returns all lowercase characters	`"Hi".lower()`	`"hi"`
`string.capitalize()`	Capitalizes first letter, lowercases remaining letters	`"wake UP".capitalize()`	`"Wake up"`
`string.strip()`	Removes leading and trailing whitespaces	`" Ny ".strip()`	`"Ny"`

String formatting with %

To insert variable values into strings shown to the user, you can use the string format operator %. Inserted into the string definition, %d is used to specify integers, %s is used to specify strings, and the variables to format (mapping key) are specified in parenthesis after the string is defined. See the example code and result below:

Code:

```
yearofbirth = 1990
pplinroom = 20
name = "Mary"
print "Your year of birth is %d. Is this correct?" % (yearofbirth)
print 'Your year of birth is %d. Is this correct?' % (yearofbirth)
print "There are %d women in the room born in %d and %s is one of them." % (pplinroom/2,
    yearofbirth, name)
```

Result:

```
Your year of birth is 1990. Is this correct?
Your year of birth is 1990. Is this correct?
There are 10 women in the room born in 1990 and Mary is one of them.
```

The first string used double quotes and the variable was inserted into the string and displayed to the user. The second string behaved just like the first string, because unlike in Ruby, defining strings with single quotes does not affect the string formatting. The third string shows that code can be evaluated (`pplinroom / 2`) and inserted into the string.

TECHNICAL STUFF

The `string.format()` method is another way to format strings in Python.

Building a Simple Tip Calculator Using Python

Practice your Python online using the Codecademy website. Codecademy is a free website created in 2011 to allow anyone to learn how to code right in the browser, without installing or downloading any software. Practice all of the tags (and a few more) that you learned in this chapter by following these steps:

1. **Open your browser, go to** www.dummies.com/go/codingfd, **and click on the link to Codecademy.**

2. **Sign in to your Codecademy account.**

Signing up is discussed in Chapter 3. Creating an account allows you to save your progress as you work, but it's optional.

3. **Navigate to and click on Python Syntax to practice some basic Python commands.**

4. **Background information is presented in the upper left portion of the site, and instructions are presented in the lower left portion of the site.**

5. **Complete the instructions in the main coding window.**

6. **After you have finished completing the instructions, click the Save and Submit Code button.**

If you have followed the instructions correctly, a green checkmark appears and you proceed to the next exercise. If an error exists in your code a warning appears with a suggested fix. If you run into a problem, or have a bug you cannot fix, click on the hint, use the Q&A Forum, or tweet me at @nikhilgabraham and include hashtag #codingFD.

5

The Part of Tens

IN THIS PART . . .

Continue to learn how to code with online resources.

Stay up to date with industry news and community discussion.

Solve coding bugs with online and offline resources.

Keep in mind ten tips as you learn how to code.

Chapter 15

Ten Free Resources for Coding and Coders

The technology world is constantly evolving. New technologies are invented, developers build new products using these technologies, and new markets emerge from people using these products. In the time it took me to write these chapters and for this book to find its way into your hands, much has already changed. The following resources help you continue learning, answer questions, and stay abreast of these changes.

The resources listed below are all completely free. Many of these resources stay free by depending on community members like you to contribute, so don't be shy about participating!

Learning-to-Code Websites

Learning to code is a constant journey that never ends for even the most experienced programmers. New languages and frameworks appear every day, and the only way to stay current is to keep learning. Although you may not be an experienced developer just yet, the following resources appeal to beginners with different learning styles. You can learn general introductory computer science topics or specific web development techniques by reading text or watching video lectures, and do it at your own pace or in a scheduled class. Let's get started!

Codecademy

www.codecademy.com

Codecademy, created for people with no previous programming experience, is the easiest way to learn how to code online. Many chapters in this book use lessons from the site. You can use the site to

>> Learn front-end languages like HTML, CSS, and JavaScript

>> Try back-end languages like Ruby, Python, and PHP

>> Build real pages from websites like AirBnb, Flipboard, and Etsy

REMEMBER

Front-end languages address website appearance, whereas back-end languages add website logic, such as what to show users and when. See Chapter 2 for more detail.

You don't need to download or install anything to start coding at Codecademy — just sign up or sign in and start learning.

TIP

If you get stuck, check for a hint at the bottom of the instructions, or click the Q&A Forum link to ask a question or to see if someone has already posted a solution to your problem.

Coursera and Udacity

www.coursera.org

www.udacity.com

MOOCs, or *massive open online courses*, are classes or courses that are taught via the Internet to a virtually unlimited number of students. These courses encourage the use of online forums and interactivity to create a sense of community. Coursera and Udacity, two of the biggest MOOCs, have a variety of coding-related courses. Each course is taught through a series of video lectures by a university faculty member or an industry expert. (See Figure 15-1.) After watching video lectures, your homework assignments and projects help reinforce what you've learned. Each site offers optional paid features, such as certificates of completion or individual support, but you don't have to pay anything to access the base material. The strength of these sites is their hundreds of hours of video dedicated to technology topics such as front-end web development, mobile web development, data science, or general computer science theory.

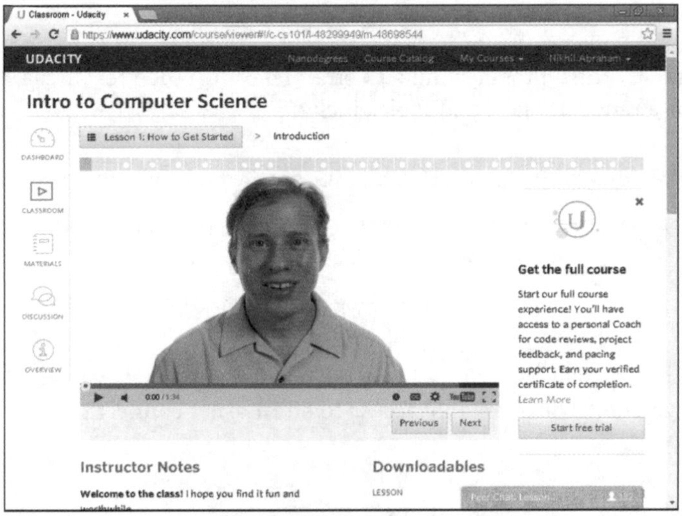

FIGURE 15-1: Intro to Computer Science, taught by University of Virginia Professor David Evans on Udacity.

TIP

Before you start a course at either website, make sure you can set aside time for study each week. You can expect to devote 5 to 10 hours per week for 7 to 10 weeks for any of these courses.

Hackdesign.org

`www.hackdesign.org`

The other half of coding is designing. Good visual design is often the difference between having hundreds of people use and share your website and having millions of people do so. Hack Design has 50 design lessons created by top designers from around the world, including designers from Facebook, Dropbox, and Google. Each lesson is emailed to you weekly, and includes articles to read, and design tasks to complete based on what you have just learned. Topics covered include typography, product design, user interactions, and rapid prototyping tools.

TIP

Many of the expert designers have public portfolio websites at which you can see past designs and projects. In addition, many post their creative work on Dribble, available at `www.dribbble.com` (note the three b's in the URL).

Code.org

`www.code.org`

In December 2013, Code.org made history when over 15 million U.S. school students participated in a learn-to-code event called Hour of Code. Throughout 2014, an additional 25 million students would practice their programming skills for one hour. Code.org hosts its own content for students from kindergarten to eighth grade. It also provides links to other learn-to-code resources, which are targeted for a range of ages, and topics include

>> Tutorials that teach HTML, JavaScript, Python, and other languages

>> Visual programming tools that help elementary and middle school students drag-and-drop their way to learning how to code

>> Instructions to make your own Angry Birds, Flappy Bird, and Lost in Space apps

TIP

Code.org also has offline learn-to-code materials, so you can keep learning even if you don't have reliable access to an Internet connection.

Coding-Reference Websites

As you learn to code, either by reading this book or from some of the websites discussed previously, you will get stuck. Your code just won't behave as you intended. This happens to every programmer — it's an inevitable part of the process of turning human logic and fuzzy thoughts into rigid code a computer can understand. The important thing is to have a plan, and to have some resources to help debug your code and solve your problem. The following resources include reference texts, which help you check your coding syntax, and community user groups, which help you check your program logic.

W3Schools

www.w3schools.com

W3Schools is one of the best resources for beginners who are just starting to learn. The website includes reference material and basic tutorials for HTML, CSS, JavaScript, PHP, and other programming languages, libraries, and standards. (See Figure 15-2.) In addition, the reference pages include many coding examples, which you can view and modify in your browser, along with a list of attributes or properties that can be used. If you know you can insert an image using HTML, change the text color using CSS, or show an alert to the user using JavaScript, but you cannot remember the exact syntax to do so, try starting with W3Schools.

TECHNICAL STUFF

Although it's a great resource, W3Schools has no affiliation with or endorsement from the W3C, which is the governing body that creates the standards browsers follow when rendering HTML, CSS, and other languages and formats.

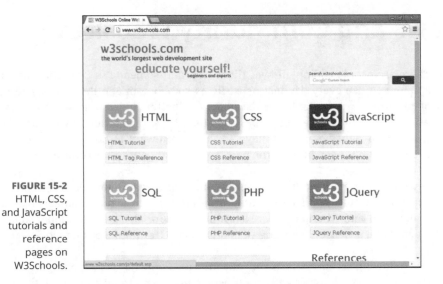

Mozilla Developer Network

http://developer.mozilla.org

Mozilla Developer Network (MDN) is a wiki-style reference and tutorial website that covers HTML, CSS, JavaScript, and various APIs. The website is maintained by the developer community, so anyone can contribute — even you! Although not as beginner-friendly as W3Schools, MDN is one of the most complete and accurate sources of documentation for web languages. Developers frequently use MDN to reference syntax, and also to see desktop and mobile browser compatibility for specific tags and commands. You can also check out tutorials on MDN hosted by the Mozilla Foundation, a non-profit organization that helps support and maintain the Firefox browser.

Stack Overflow

www.stackoverflow.com

Stack Overflow is relatively young, founded in 2008, but has quickly become the best place for developers to ask and answer questions about coding. Anyone can ask a question, individual programmers provide answers, and the website community votes up or down the answers to show agreement or disagreement. The site includes topics that cover all major web programming languages, and the most popular topics include JavaScript, Ruby, and Python.

TIP

Before asking a question, search the website and see if an answer to your question has already been posted. One of the website rules of etiquette is showing you have done some research before posting a question.

Tech News and Community Websites

There are people coding all over the world, and someone in Shanghai can make an app you use every day just as easily as someone in San Francisco. A number of resources are available for developers to better understand what others are working on, both at big companies and at startups. In addition to what people are working on right now, if you have a website you want to build, it can be helpful to see what has been built in the past, so you can identify areas for improvement.

Beyond being informative, these resources offer communities of people with goals similar to yours. These communities are among the most valuable resources available to you. Whether you are learning to code or an expert developer soliciting feedback on a website, working with others is better than working alone.

The following resources help you stay informed on what is happening in the tech community, and interact with other people interested in tech in your city.

TechCrunch

www.techcrunch.com

TechCrunch is a popular blog that covers technology startups and major technology companies. In 2006, the website cemented its reputation when it broke the story of Google acquiring YouTube for $1.6 billion. Along with its online reporting, TechCrunch has conferences throughout the year, such as Disrupt, which hosts conversations with industry veterans and highlights new tech startups.

TIP

TechCrunch also operates CrunchBase (www.crunchbase.com), a crowdsourced database of 650,000 people and companies. Crunchbase is one of the most accurate and complete sources of information on startups, past and present, and their founders.

Hacker News

http://news.ycombinator.com

HackerNews (HN) is a discussion website hosted by YCombinator, a startup incubator in California. The website homepage is a collection of hyperlinks, often to startup websites and news articles, that individual users have submitted. (See Figure 15-3.) After a submission is made, the entire community can upvote the submission, and the top-ranked submissions are listed first on the homepage. Also, the community can comment on individual submissions, and each comment can also be upvoted, with the top-ranked comment appearing first on each submission page. In this way, the community curates the best news, which appears on the front page, and the best comments, which appear on each submission page. The community is made up of hundreds of thousands of users, including AirBnB co-founder Brian Chesky, Dropbox co-founder Drew Houston, Netscape co-founder and now venture capitalist Marc Andreessen, and venture capitalist Fred Wilson.

FIGURE 15-3:
The community-curated news and discussions at HackerNews homepage.

TIP Submission titles that begin with "Show HN" are a request to the community to comment on a startup website that has just launched. Submission titles that begin with "Ask HN" are a request to the community to answer or comment on a question.

Meetup

www.meetup.com

Meetup is a website that organizes face-to-face local meetings based on interests or activities. Meetup organizers, who are volunteer community members, host meetings by posting information on the website. Then, community members search, join, and RSVP for meetings through the website.

To use the website, go to www.meetup.com and then follow these steps:

1. **Enter your city and how far you are willing to travel.**

2. **In the search field, enter *coding* or *web development*. If you have a specific language you want to learn, like Ruby or JavaScript, enter the language name.**

3. **Review the Meetup groups, and look for ones with a good number of members. You can join a group and receive notifications of future events, or RSVP for a specific upcoming event. Some events may have a fee to cover expenses.**

Although you can learn alone, finding other people learning to code is a great way to stay motivated and keep up your momentum. The people you meet may be learning to code for the same reasons you are, such as to build a website, improve skills for an existing job, or find a new tech-related job.

Chapter 16

Ten Tips for Novice Coders

Learning to code is more popular today than ever before. It seems like everyone has a website or an app idea, and as soon as your friends, family, or coworkers discover your new coding abilities, many will ask for advice and help. No matter whether you're dabbling at it after work, or attending an intensive ten-week coding boot camp, learning to code can be a challenging journey. It can pay to pick up a few pointers from some of the people who crossed the finish line ahead of you. Keep the following tips in mind, especially when starting your coding journey.

Pick a Language, Any Language

As a novice coder, you may not be sure where to start. Should you learn C++, Python, Java, Ruby, PHP, JavaScript all at the same time, sequentially, or just pick a few? If you have never programmed before, I recommend learning a language used to create web pages, because with these languages it's easy to get started and publish work for others to see. Within this set of languages, I recommend starting with HTML and CSS. Both are markup languages, which are the easiest to learn, and let you put content on a web page with HTML, and style that content with CSS. After you understand some of the basics of presenting content, you can then learn a programming language to manipulate that content. Keep in mind that you don't need to learn every programming language — JavaScript, which adds interactivity to the web page, is a common starting point for beginners, along with either Ruby or Python, which adds more advanced features like user accounts and logins.

Learning to code is similar to learning to drive a car. When you first learned to drive, you probably didn't worry too much about the type of car you were driving. After passing the driving test, you could operate just about any car, even one you hadn't driven before, because you knew to look for the ignition, accelerator, and brake. Learning a programming language works the same way: After you learn one language, you know what to look for, and learning and using another language becomes easier. In other words, just start somewhere!

Define a Goal

When you start learning to code, picking a goal can help you stay motivated. You can pick any goal you like, but make sure it's something you would be really excited to accomplish. Good goals for beginners include

>> Creating a small website — consisting of one to four different pages — for yourself, a business, or a group.

>> Building your coding vocabulary so you can understand what developers or designers say in meetings at work.

>> Creating a prototype, or a basic version, of a website or app idea — for example, an app that tells you when the next bus is arriving to your current location.

At first, practice doing very small coding tasks — the equivalent of chopping vegetables in culinary school. These tasks, such as bolding a headline, may leave you feeling disconnected from your ultimate goal. But as you keep learning, you will start to piece together individual coding skills and see a path to accomplish your goal.

TIP

Pick a simple goal at first to build your confidence and technical skills. As you gain confidence, you can build more professional-looking websites and apps.

Break Down Your Goal into Bite-Sized Steps

After defining a goal, break it down into small steps. This helps you

>> See all the steps needed to complete the goal

>> Research how to do each specific step

>> Ask others for help easily when you're stuck on a step

For example, if you want to build an app that tells you when you can expect the next bus to arrive closest to your current location, you can list the steps as follows:

1. Find your current location.

2. Find the bus station closest to your current location.

3. Identify the specific bus that travels to the closest bus station.

4. Determine the location of that bus traveling to the bus station.

5. Calculate the distance from the bus's current location to the bus station.

6. Assuming an average speed for the bus, convert the distance into time using the equation distance = speed × time.

7. Display the time to the user.

This level of detail is specific enough to start researching individual steps, such as how to find your current location using code, and it gives you a complete list of steps from start to finish for the intended goal.

TIP

At first, the steps you create may be broad or incomplete, but with time you will improve your ability to detail these steps, which are sometimes called *specifications*.

Distinguish Cupcake from Frosting

Whether you're at home creating your first app, or at work on a team building a website, your projects will tend to include too many features to build by a specific deadline. This leads inevitably to one of three results: The project launches on time but is buggy; the project launches late; or your team works overtime to launch the project on time. The only other choices for a project behind schedule are to extend the deadline, which usually does not happen, or to add additional programmers, which usually is not helpful because of the time needed to get the new programmers up-to-speed.

A better strategy is to decide upfront which features are the cupcake — that is, which are essential — and which are the unessential frosting, the ones that are nice to have but optional. This shows you where your priorities are. If your project is running over on time or budget, you can build the optional features later or not at all.

When building your own apps make sure you distinguish the essential from the optional features before you actually start coding. In the bus app example above, determining my current location could be optional. Instead, I could select one specific bus stop, and first complete steps 3 through 7. Then, if time allows, I can make the app more flexible by finding my current location, and then finding the closest bus stop.

TIP

The phrase *minimum viable product* is used by developers to refer to the set of features essential to the proper functioning of the product.

Google Is a Developer's Best Friend

Developers constantly use the Google search engine to research either general questions on how to code a feature, or specific questions on syntax for a command or tag. For example, imagine that a few months from now, after reading this book, you need to add an image to a website. You remember that HTML has a tag to insert images on a website, but you don't recall the exact syntax. To quickly and efficiently find the answer, you could follow these steps:

1. **Go to** www.google.com.

2. **Search for** HTML image syntax.

   The programming language, the intended command, and the word *syntax* should be sufficient to find a good set of resources.

3. **For syntax questions in HTML and CSS, you will likely see these domains names in the top 10 search results, and you should read their content as a next step:**

   - w3schools.com is one of the best resources for beginners to find basic information.

   - developer.mozilla.org is a crowdsourced documentation and tutorial site. Its documentation is very accurate, although some content is not beginner-friendly.

- `stackexchange.com` and `stackoverflow.com` are crowdsourced discussion sites where developers can ask and answer questions.

- `w3.org` is the governing body that creates HTML and CSS standards. Its documentation is the most accurate, but it's dry and not beginner-friendly.

You can use this same process to research questions in other coding languages, or to find code examples from other developers who are building features similar to yours.

Zap Those Bugs

While you're doing all this coding you will inevitably create errors, commonly referred to as *bugs*. There are three types of errors:

>> **Syntax errors** occur when you write invalid code the computer doesn't understand. For example, in CSS, you'd write `color: blue;` to change the color of an element. If you wrote `font-color: blue;` instead, you'd generate a syntax error because `font-color` is an invalid property.

>> **Semantic errors** occur when you write valid code that has an unintended effect. For example, trying to divide a number by zero is a semantic error in JavaScript.

>> **Logic or design errors** occur when you write valid code that has the intended effect, but the code produces the wrong result. For example, in JavaScript, converting miles to feet using `var miles = 4000 * feet` is a logic error. Although the code is written correctly and does what the programmer wants it to do, it still produces the wrong answer — there are actually 5,280 feet in a mile, not 4,000.

Your browser will do its best to display your HTML or CSS code as you intended, even in the presence of syntax errors. However, with other programming languages, such as JavaScript, code with syntax errors won't run at all. The best way to find and eliminate bugs is to first check your code syntax, and then the logic. Review your code line by line, and if you still cannot find the error, ask another person to take a look at your code, or post it on an online community forum like `stackoverflow.com`.

TIP

Developers use specialized tools in the browser to diagnose and debug errors. You can learn more about these developer tools in the Chrome browser by going to `www.codeschool.com/courses/discover-devtools`.

Just Ship It

Reid Hoffman, the founder of LinkedIn, famously said, "If you are not embarrassed by the first version of your product, you've launched too late." When you start coding, you will likely be reluctant to show others your creations, whether it's your first basic website or something more complex. Hoffman was commenting on this desire to keep trying to perfect what you have built, and says instead to release (or "ship") your code to public view even if you feel embarrassed. Regardless of the size of your website or app, it is better to receive feedback early and learn from your mistakes, then to continue heading in the wrong direction.

Also, remember that the highly trafficked, highly polished websites you use today started initially from humble beginning and very simple prototypes. Google's first homepage, for example, had only a fraction of the functionality or style of its homepage today. (See Figure 16-1.)

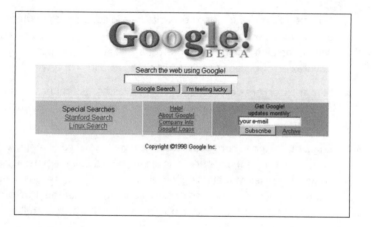

FIGURE 16-1:
Google's original homepage in 1998.

Collect Feedback

After you finish coding the first version of your website or app, collect feedback on your code and on the final product. Even if everything is working and your website looks great, that doesn't mean your code was written correctly or that your site does everything it could. For example, YouTube initially started as a video-dating site, but changed to a general video-sharing website based on user feedback.

The best way to obtain this information is to collect quantitative and qualitative data on your code and the product. Measuring the places where visitors click and how long they stay on each web page gives you quantitative information, which helps you diagnose and improve low-performing pages. You can collect qualitative information by surveying users, either by emailing them survey questions or by watching people in-person use your website and then asking questions. Often this data will surprise you — users may find confusing the features you thought were obvious and easily understood, and vice-versa. Similarly, if possible, have someone examine your code, in a process called a *code review,* to ensure that you didn't overlook any major problems.

Iterate on Your Code

After you've collected feedback, the next step is to "iterate" on that feedback: Keep coding until the major issues in your feedback have been addressed, and until you have improved both the code and the product. Keep in mind that it's usually best to confirm the usefulness of your product first, before spending time improving the code.

This process — building a product with a minimum set of essential features, collecting feedback on the product, and then iterating on that feedback — is sometimes referred to as the *Lean Startup methodology.* In the past, manufacturing processes, once set, were extremely difficult to change, but these days, changing software is as simple as modifying a few lines of code. This contrasts with the way products used to be coded, which involved longer development cycles and less upfront feedback.

TIP

Just like with document drafts, save the old versions of your code in case you realize an older version was better, or in the event you find bugs in the current version of your code and you have to use an older version of the code to debug it.

Share Your Success and Failure

While coding you may have come across documentation on a website you found confusing or just plain wrong. Maybe you found a great resource or a tool that worked especially well for a product you were building. Or perhaps the opposite happened — no one used the features you built with code, and you had to give up the project.

In all these situations, the best thing you can do for yourself and the larger community is to blog about your successes and failures. Blogging benefits you because it shows others the issues you're thinking about and trying to solve. Similarly, blogging benefits others who will use Google to search for and read about your experiences, just as you used Google to search for ideas and solve problems. Many non-technical entrepreneurs, such as Dennis Crowley of Foursquare and Kevin Systrom of Instagram, taught themselves enough coding to build small working prototypes, built successful products, and then shared that journey with others.

TIP

You can blog for free and share your experiences using blogging sites like Wordpress (www.wordpress.com), Blogger (www.blogger.com), or Tumblr (www.tumblr.com).

Index

Symbols

! (exclamation point) (Ruby), 203

!= (inequality) operator

  JavaScript, 141

  Python, 221

  Ruby, 207

(comment symbol) (Python), 219

#{...} (hashtag sequence) (Ruby), 210–211

( ) (parenthesis) (JavaScript), 138, 147

** (exponentiation) operator

  Python, 218

  Ruby, 204

. (period)

  HTML, 108

  Ruby, 203

/ (forward slash) (HTML), 45, 54

: (colon)

  CSS, 79, 87

  Python, 217, 221

; (semi-colon)

  CSS, 79

  JavaScript, 138

? (question mark) (Ruby), 202

\' or \" (quotation mark escape sequences)

  Python, 220

  Ruby, 206

\n (newline escape sequence)

  Python, 220, 223

  Ruby, 206, 208

\t (tab escape sequence)

  Python, 220

  Ruby, 206

_ (underscore)

  Python, 218

  Ruby, 204

{ } (curly brackets; braces)

  CSS, 78–79, 195

  JavaScript, 138, 140, 147, 195

+ (concatenation) operator (JavaScript), 147

< > (angle brackets), 45–46, 195

< (less than) operator

  JavaScript, 141

  Python, 221

  Ruby, 207

<= (less than or equal to) operator

  JavaScript, 141

  Python, 221

  Ruby, 207

= (equals sign)

  HTML, 47

  JavaScript, 139

  Ruby, 204

== (equality) operator

  Python, 221

  Ruby, 207

=== (equality) operator (JavaScript), 141, 143

> (greater than) operator

  JavaScript, 141

  Python, 221

  Ruby, 207

>= (greater than or equal to) operator

  JavaScript, 141

  Python, 221

  Ruby, 207

" " (quotes)

  CSS, 86

  HTML, 46–47, 68

  JavaScript, 138

A

a element and tags (HTML), 53

A/B testing, 61

ABC, 213

Abraham, Nik, 2

.abs method (Ruby), 205

abs(*n*) function (Python), 219

action attribute (HTML), 72

active state (CSS), 86–88

ad blockers, 24

Adobe Photoshop, 36

D

E

greater than (>) operator
JavaScript, 141
Python, 221
Ruby, 207
greater than or equal to (>=) operator
JavaScript, 141
Python, 221
Ruby, 207
Groupon, 11

H

h1 element and tags (HTML), 45–46, 51, 189
h2 element and tags (HTML), 51
h3 element and tags (HTML), 51
h4 element and tags (HTML), 51
h5 element and tags (HTML), 51
h6 element and tags (HTML), 51
Hackdesign.org, 231
HackerNews (HN), 234–235
hashtag sequence (#{...}) (Ruby), 210–211
Haversine formula, 192
head element and tags (HTML), 48–49, 189
heading tags (HTML), 49–51
HealthCare.gov, 35
height attribute (HTML), 68–70
height property (CSS), 113–114
hex codes, 84
hidden attribute (HTML), 45–46
high-level programming languages, 15
Hipmunk, 60
HN (HackerNews), 234–235
Hoffman, Reid, 242
Hook Model, 13
Hopper, Grace, 38, 54
Horse ebooks, 105
hotlinking, 54, 89
Hotmail, 10
Hour of Code event, 231–232
Houston, Drew, 159, 235
hover state (CSS), 86–88
href attribute (HTML), 52, 86, 94

HTML (Hypertext Markup Language)
adding CSS to, 76–77, 92–94
for building mobile web apps, 29
Codecademy tutorial, 57–58, 73
coding simple websites with, 27
common tags
headings, 49–51
hyperlinks, 50, 52–53
images, 50, 53–54
paragraphs, 50–52
forms
creating basic, 71–73
function of, 70–71
as front-end language, 26
function of, 43–44
history of, 58
HTML5, 47–48, 58
inspecting and changing code, 20–22
lists
nesting, 62–63
ordered, 62
overview, 61
unordered, 62
pre-written code, 189–190
structure of
attributes, 46–47
elements, 45–46
general discussion, 44–49
tags, 45–46, 48–49
tables
aligning tables and cells, 67–70
overview, 63–64
sizing columns and rows, 66–67
structure of, 64–65
text
bold, 55–56
general discussion, 54–55
italics, 55–56
strikethrough, 55–56
superscript and subscript, 56
underline, 55–56
website readability, 59–61

tech news and community websites, 234–236

TechCrunch, 180, 234

text editors, 39, 57

text-align property (CSS), 102

text-decoration property (CSS), 82, 86–87

TextEdit, 39

TextMate 2.0, 39, 57

th element and tags (HTML), 65

Thornton, Jacob, 119, 167

Time Magazine, 12

title attribute (HTML), 45–46

title element and tags (HTML), 48–49

.toFixed(*n*) method (JavaScript), 145

tooltips, 45

Torvalds, Linus, 187

.toUpperCase( ) method (JavaScript), 201

tr element and tags (HTML), 65, 68–69

Tumblr, 245

Twitter. *See also* Bootstrap
  author's account, 2, 40
  Ruby, 200
  Share button, 27
  use of code in public relations, 12

type attribute (HTML), 71, 148

U

u element and tags (HTML), 55

Uber, 7, 11

Udacity, 230–231

ul element and tags (HTML), 62

ul selector (CSS), 98

underlined text (HTML), 55–56

underscore (_)
  Python, 218
  Ruby, 204

unordered lists (HTML), 62, 98

upcase method (Ruby), 210

.upper( ) function (Python), 224

user input
  collecting and displaying output
    Python, 222–223
    Ruby, 208–209
  prompting for (JavaScript), 146
  removing whitespace from (Ruby), 210

user interface/user experience (UI/UX) designers, 165

user-generated coding websites, 181

V

valign attribute (HTML), 68–70

value attribute (HTML), 71

values
  CSS
    auto, 90
    contain, 90
    cover, 90
    cursive, 78, 85
    fantasy, 85
    fixed, 91–92
    monospace, 85
    no-repeat, 91
    repeat, 91
    repeat-x, 91
    repeat-y, 91
    sans-serif, 85
    scroll, 91–92
    serif, 85
  HTML
    GET, 72
    mailto, 72
    POST, 72

Van Rossum, Guido, 14, 213, 216

var keyword (JavaScript), 139–140

variables
  JavaScript
    Boolean data type, 140–144
    case sensitivity, 140
    changing value of, 140
    declaring, 139–140
    numbers data type, 144–145
    storing data, 139–140
    strings data type, 144–145
  Python
    Boolean data type, 221–222
    case sensitivity, 218
    declaring, 218
    defined, 217–218
    numbers data type, 218–220
    strings data type, 220

About the Author

Nikhil Abraham has worked at Codecademy.com for the last two years. At Codecademy, he helps technology, finance, media, and advertising companies teach their employees how to code. With his help, thousands of marketing, sales, and recruiting professionals have written their first lines of code and built functional applications. In addition to teaching, he manages partnerships and business development for Codecademy, and has helped bring coding to schools in the United States, Brazil, Argentina, France, and the United Kingdom.

Prior to Codecademy, Nikhil worked in a variety of fields, including management consulting, investment banking, and law, and founded a Y-Combinator–backed technology education startup. He received a JD and MBA from the University of Chicago, and a BA in quantitative economics from Tufts University.

Nikhil lives in Manhattan, New York.

Dedication

This book is dedicated to Molly Grovak.

Author's Acknowledgments

This book was possible with help from a number of people.

Thanks to all the people at Wiley, including Steven Hayes, for keeping an open mind to as many ideas as can fit in one phone call, and Christopher Morris for edits and helpful advice. Also, thank you to all the technical editorial, layout, and graphics folks for turning text of variable quality into text of outstanding quality.

Thanks to those of you who helped shape the content in this book and online. For everyone at Codecademy, including Zach and Ryan, thank you for the feedback on the chapters and for answering my questions. Thanks to Douglas Rushkoff, for starting a national conversation on whether we as a society should program or be programmed, and for bringing this message to schools, universities, and non-profits. Thanks to Susan Kish, for being the only executive I can find who has spoken publicly about her journey learning how to code (check out her TED Talk!), and for seeing the future of coding in corporations. Thanks to Alia Shafir and Joshua Slusarz for all the coding sessions you helped organize, leaders you wrangled, rooms you reserved, and laptops you rebooted. Thanks to Melissa Frescholtz and her leadership team for supporting a culture of code, and bringing code education even to places where it's used every day. Thanks to alumni at Cornell University, Northwestern University, University of Virginia, and Yale University for testing early versions of content, and helping make it better. Thanks to the people at Donorschoose.org, including Charles Best and Ali Austerlitz, and at Google.org for shining a bright light on coding for women and girls. Thanks to Code.org for making coding accessible and cool for tens of millions of kids in the United States and abroad.

Finally, thanks to Molly, who ordered more take-out, brewed more tea, and cleaned the apartment more times than I can count.

Publisher's Acknowledgments

Executive Editor: Steve Hayes
Senior Project Editor: Christopher Morris
Copy Editor: Christopher Morris
Technical Editor: Travis Faas
Editorial Assistant: Claire Johnson
Sr. Editorial Assistant: Cherie Case

Production Editor: Melissa Cossell
Cover Image: ©iinspiration/Shutterstock

Apple & Mac

iPad For Dummies,
6th Edition
978-1-118-72306-7

iPhone For Dummies,
7th Edition
978-1-118-69083-3

Macs All-in-One
For Dummies, 4th Edition
978-1-118-82210-4

OS X Mavericks
For Dummies
978-1-118-69188-5

Blogging & Social Media

Facebook For Dummies,
5th Edition
978-1-118-63312-0

Social Media Engagement
For Dummies
978-1-118-53019-1

WordPress For Dummies,
6th Edition
978-1-118-79161-5

Business

Stock Investing
For Dummies, 4th Edition
978-1-118-37678-2

Investing For Dummies,
6th Edition
978-0-470-90545-6

Personal Finance
For Dummies, 7th Edition
978-1-118-11785-9

QuickBooks 2014
For Dummies
978-1-118-72005-9

Small Business Marketing
Kit For Dummies,
3rd Edition
978-1-118-31183-7

Careers

Job Interviews
For Dummies, 4th Edition
978-1-118-11290-8

Job Searching with Social
Media For Dummies,
2nd Edition
978-1-118-67856-5

Personal Branding
For Dummies
978-1-118-11792-7

Resumes For Dummies,
6th Edition
978-0-470-87361-8

Starting an Etsy Business
For Dummies, 2nd Edition
978-1-118-59024-9

Diet & Nutrition

Belly Fat Diet For Dummies
978-1-118-34585-6

Mediterranean Diet
For Dummies
978-1-118-71525-3

Nutrition For Dummies,
5th Edition
978-0-470-93231-5

Digital Photography

Digital SLR Photography
All-in-One For Dummies,
2nd Edition
978-1-118-59082-9

Digital SLR Video &
Filmmaking For Dummies
978-1-118-36598-4

Photoshop Elements 12
For Dummies
978-1-118-72714-0

Gardening

Herb Gardening
For Dummies, 2nd Edition
978-0-470-61778-6

Gardening with Free-Range
Chickens For Dummies
978-1-118-54754-0

Health

Boosting Your Immunity
For Dummies
978-1-118-40200-9

Diabetes For Dummies,
4th Edition
978-1-118-29447-5

Living Paleo For Dummies
978-1-118-29405-5

Big Data

Big Data For Dummies
978-1-118-50422-2

Data Visualization
For Dummies
978-1-118-50289-1

Hadoop For Dummies
978-1-118-60755-8

Language &
Foreign Language

500 Spanish Verbs
For Dummies
978-1-118-02382-2

English Grammar
For Dummies, 2nd Edition
978-0-470-54664-2

French All-in-One
For Dummies
978-1-118-22815-9

German Essentials
For Dummies
978-1-118-18422-6

Italian For Dummies,
2nd Edition
978-1-118-00465-4

Available in print and e-book formats.

Available wherever books are sold. **For more information or to order direct visit www.dummies.com**

Math & Science

Algebra I For Dummies,
2nd Edition
978-0-470-55964-2

Anatomy and Physiology
For Dummies, 2nd Edition
978-0-470-92326-9

Astronomy For Dummies,
3rd Edition
978-1-118-37697-3

Biology For Dummies,
2nd Edition
978-0-470-59875-7

Chemistry For Dummies,
2nd Edition
978-1-118-00730-3

1001 Algebra II Practice
Problems For Dummies
978-1-118-44662-1

Microsoft Office

Excel 2013 For Dummies
978-1-118-51012-4

Office 2013 All-in-One
For Dummies
978-1-118-51636-2

PowerPoint 2013
For Dummies
978-1-118-50253-2

Word 2013 For Dummies
978-1-118-49123-2

Music

Blues Harmonica
For Dummies
978-1-118-25269-7

Guitar For Dummies,
3rd Edition
978-1-118-11554-1

iPod & iTunes
For Dummies, 10th Edition
978-1-118-50864-0

Programming

Beginning Programming
with C For Dummies
978-1-118-73763-7

Excel VBA Programming
For Dummies, 3rd Edition
978-1-118-49037-2

Java For Dummies,
6th Edition
978-1-118-40780-6

Religion & Inspiration

The Bible For Dummies
978-0-7645-5296-0

Buddhism For Dummies,
2nd Edition
978-1-118-02379-2

Catholicism For Dummies,
2nd Edition
978-1-118-07778-8

Self-Help & Relationships

Beating Sugar Addiction
For Dummies
978-1-118-54645-1

Meditation For Dummies,
3rd Edition
978-1-118-29144-3

Seniors

Laptops For Seniors
For Dummies, 3rd Edition
978-1-118-71105-7

Computers For Seniors
For Dummies, 3rd Edition
978-1-118-11553-4

iPad For Seniors
For Dummies, 6th Edition
978-1-118-72826-0

Social Security
For Dummies
978-1-118-20573-0

Smartphones & Tablets

Android Phones
For Dummies, 2nd Edition
978-1-118-72030-1

Nexus Tablets
For Dummies
978-1-118-77243-0

Samsung Galaxy S 4
For Dummies
978-1-118-64222-1

Samsung Galaxy Tabs
For Dummies
978-1-118-77294-2

Test Prep

ACT For Dummies,
5th Edition
978-1-118-01259-8

ASVAB For Dummies,
3rd Edition
978-0-470-63760-9

GRE For Dummies,
7th Edition
978-0-470-88921-3

Officer Candidate Tests
For Dummies
978-0-470-59876-4

Physician's Assistant Exam
For Dummies
978-1-118-11556-5

Series 7 Exam For Dummies
978-0-470-09932-2

Windows 8

Windows 8.1 All-in-One
For Dummies
978-1-118-82087-2

Windows 8.1 For Dummies
978-1-118-82121-3

Windows 8.1 For Dummies,
Book + DVD Bundle
978-1-118-82107-7

ℯ Available in print and e-book formats.

Available wherever books are sold. **For more information or to order direct visit www.dummies.com**

Take Dummies with you everywhere you go!

Whether you are excited about e-books, want more from the web, must have your mobile apps, or are swept up in social media, Dummies makes everything easier.

Visit Us
bit.ly/JE0O

Like Us
on.fb.me/1f1ThNu

Follow Us
bit.ly/ZDytkR

Watch Us
bit.ly/gbOQHn

Join Us
linkd.in/1gurkMm

Pin Us
bit.ly/16caOLd

Circle Us
bit.ly/1aQTuDQ

Shop Us
bit.ly/4dEp9

Leverage the Power

For Dummies is the global leader in the reference category and one of the most trusted and highly regarded brands in the world. No longer just focused on books, customers now have access to the For Dummies content they need in the format they want. Let us help you develop a solution that will fit your brand and help you connect with your customers.

Advertising & Sponsorships

Connect with an engaged audience on a powerful multimedia site, and position your message alongside expert how-to content.

Targeted ads • Video • Email marketing • Microsites • Sweepstakes sponsorship

Custom Publishing

Reach a global audience in any language by creating a solution that will differentiate you from competitors, amplify your message, and encourage customers to make a buying decision.

Apps • Books • eBooks • Video • Audio • Webinars

Brand Licensing & Content

Leverage the strength of the world's most popular reference brand to reach new audiences and channels of distribution.

For more information, visit www.Dummies.com/biz

Dummies products make life easier!

- DIY
- Consumer Electronics
- Crafts
- Software
- Cookware
- Hobbies
- Videos
- Music
- Games
- and More!

For more info ... store by category.

FOR
DUMMIES
A Wiley Brand